Getting Started with Ghost

Reach out to the world and publish great content
with the power of Ghost

Kezz Bracey

David Balderston

Andy Boutte

[PACKT] open source *
PUBLISHING   community experience distilled

BIRMINGHAM - MUMBAI

Getting Started with Ghost

First published: November 2014

Production reference: 1191114

Published by Packt Publishing Ltd.
Livery Place
35 Livery Street
Birmingham B3 2PB, UK.

ISBN 978-1-78398-518-0

www.packtpub.com

Cover image by Benoit Benedetti (benoit.benedetti@gmail.com)

Credits

About the Authors

Kezz Bracey is a web designer and frontend developer from Australia who has been working in the field for the better part of a decade. Theme development kicked off for her in the early days on the Joomla! platform, moving on to creating themes and plugins for WordPress, and she began designing themes for the Ghost blogging platform at its release.

David Balderston had early access to Ghost and started `www.howtoinstallghost.com/` with Andy Boutte. From there, he helped to launch other sites related to Ghost, including `www.ghostforbeginners.com`, `www.allaboutghost.com/`, and `www.allghostthemes.com/`. His background in IT helped with troubleshooting problems and portraying them in a way people can clearly understand. He has been around Ghost from the very beginning and has helped many people install and use the Ghost platform.

Andy Boutte worked in the Apple industry for 5 years where he received a dozen certifications and became an Apple certified computer technician and iPhone technician. He currently works for a leading software company, Shopatron, as a DevOps engineer and previously worked there as a quality assurance analyst. This led him to testing Ghost before its initial release and he began writing on `www.howtoinstallghost.com` and `www.allaboutghost.com`. With his experience, he has developed the unique skill of breaking down technical topics into terms that are easy to understand, which he utilizes in his writing today.

About the Reviewers

İsmail Demirbilek is a software engineer and web enthusiast living in İstanbul, Turkey. He is working with cutting-edge web technologies since his college days at Istanbul Technical University back in 2012. He is mainly focused on frontend engineering besides being a Big Data search engineer at Egemsoft.

He is also an open source maintainer. He has published many projects in terms of giving back to the community. He is currently working on several web projects.

Gabor Javorszky is one of the core developers on Ghost. He's been in the web industry for the past 10 years. It all started with a bespoke Flash website for an event and a forum he's written by hand. Later on, WordPress became the tool of his choice with a small sidestep to another CMS while working at an agency. Everything he knows he learned all by himself, reading articles, trying, and building things, and figuring out what works and how.

Currently he is the senior developer at Electric Studio, a small WordPress only web design agency in Oxfordshire, the United Kingdom.

He has also reviewed *Getting Started with Zurb Foundation 4* for Packt Publishing earlier this year.

I'd like to thank the entire team at Ghost for helping me through the obscure code parts, especially Hannah Wolfe! I'd also like to thank the team at Packt Publishing for guiding me through the book review process.

www.PacktPub.com

Support files, eBooks, discount offers, and more

For support files and downloads related to your book, please visit www.PacktPub.com.

Did you know that Packt offers eBook versions of every book published, with PDF and ePub files available? You can upgrade to the eBook version at www.PacktPub.com and as a print book customer, you are entitled to a discount on the eBook copy. Get in touch with us at service@packtpub.com for more details.

At www.PacktPub.com, you can also read a collection of free technical articles, sign up for a range of free newsletters and receive exclusive discounts and offers on Packt books and eBooks.

https://www2.packtpub.com/books/subscription/packtlib

Do you need instant solutions to your IT questions? PacktLib is Packt's online digital book library. Here, you can search, access, and read Packt's entire library of books.

Why subscribe?

- Fully searchable across every book published by Packt
- Copy and paste, print, and bookmark content
- On demand and accessible via a web browser

Free access for Packt account holders

If you have an account with Packt at www.PacktPub.com, you can use this to access PacktLib today and view 9 entirely free books. Simply use your login credentials for immediate access.

Table of Contents

Preface   1

Chapter 1: The First Steps with Ghost   7

Automated installation of Ghost   7
A background on Ghost's hosting   8
Using Ghost's hosting solution   8
Creating a blog on Ghost(Pro)   9
Creating your user account   9
Configure settings   11
General settings   11
User settings   12
Content management   14
The content management area   14
Creating and deleting posts   15
Converting a post to a page   15
Modifying the permalink or publishing date   16
Featured posts   17
Editing existing posts   17
The post editing area and inline preview   18
Setting the title   19
Saving a draft   19
Adding tags   19
The word count display   20
Publishing and unpublishing posts   20
Converting a post to page, plus permalink and date modification
from the post editor   22

Markdown, image upload, and inline HTML	**22**
Image upload	24
Inline HTML	25
Hosting Ghost on other providers	**25**
DigitalOcean	26
Amazon EC2	27
Summary	**28**
Chapter 2: Manual Installation and Configuration of Ghost	**29**
Manually installing Ghost on your local computer	**30**
Command-line interface and SSH access	30
Identifying your VPS operating system	31
Installing Ghost on Ubuntu (VPS and local)	32
Configuring Ghost on Ubuntu for VPS	34
Installing Ghost on CentOS (VPS and local)	34
Configuring Ghost on CentOS for VPS	36
Installing Ghost on Mac OS X (local)	37
Configuring Ghost on OS X	37
Installing Ghost on Windows (local)	39
Configuring Ghost on Windows	39
Additional configuration for VPS usage	**41**
Pointing a custom domain at Ghost (VPS)	41
Hosting multiple Ghost blogs on the same VPS	42
Nginx	42
Keeping Ghost running (VPS)	43
The forever process manager	43
Adding SSL for security	44
Upgrading Ghost	46
Troubleshooting	**47**
listen EADDRINUSE IN USE	47
listen EADDRNOTAVAIL	47
Command not found	48
Places to find help	48
Summary	**48**
Chapter 3: Preparing for Theme Development	**49**
Handlebars' logicless templating	**50**
Double and triple curly braces	51
Handlebars' paths	51
The each and foreach block helpers	52
The if helper	52
The unless and else helpers	53

Template tag parameters	54
Comments	54
Creating CSS via the Stylus preprocessor	**54**
Variables	55
Stylus syntax	56
Mixins	57
Setting up your environment	**58**
Sublime Text 2 and Package Control	58
Installing Stylus and highlighting Handlebars syntax	59
Creating your project environment	60
Installing Grunt	60
Creating a project folder	61
Installing the project compiler	61
Set project options	62
Run the watch task	62
Minifying JavaScript	63
Summary	**63**
Chapter 4: Beginning Ghost Theme Development	**65**
An overview of the currently available design options	**66**
The themeable areas of a Ghost blog	66
The primary theme design building blocks	67
Extra design tools	68
The current exclusions in Ghost	69
Quick start theme quiz	**69**
Default	70
Index and tag archive	70
Tag archive	71
Post and page	71
Post	72
Creating your theme shell	**72**
The setup file and folder structure	72
Running the first CSS and JS compile into theme	74
Adding basic code to template files and package.json	74
package.json	75
default.hbs	75
Extra notes	78
index.hbs	79
post.hbs	82
tag.hbs	84
page.hbs	85
Adding test content and activating your theme	**85**
Summary	**86**

Chapter 5: Applying Design Choices and Visual Styling ────────── 87

Stylus files — **88**
The import_stylus.styl file — 88
The meta folder — 88
The vars_mixins_etc folder — 89
The styles folder — 89
Applying the quick start theme quiz choices — **90**
The default themes — 90
Overall layout – single column — 90
Overall layout – twin column — 94
Use the blog cover image – as site background — 97
Single column layout – header height auto — 100
Single column layout – header height large — 102
Single column layout – full screen header — 104
Index and tag archive — 105
Posts – excerpt, full or trimmed — 105
If excerpt – show post's first image/video/soundcloud — 105
Adding zebra striping – alternate colors every second post — 106
Featured posts – list first above default posts — 108
Applying styles to featured posts — 109
Applying styles to the posts with certain tags — 110
Tag archive — 113
Post and page — 114
If single column layout AND header height full/large – post header style — 114
Post — 115
Adding unique visual styling — **116**
Adding icon fonts — 116
Setting image fallbacks — 117
Example design – twin column visual styling — 118
Example responsiveness – twin column design media queries — 123
Summary — **129**

Appendix: Markdown Syntax and Ghost Shortcut Keys ────────── 131

Index ────────── 133

Preface

When John O'Nolan, the founder of Ghost, first published a blog post in November 2012 describing his *idealistic and fictional concept* of a light, simple blogging engine focused entirely on content publishing, little did he know the chain reaction of events that was about to unfold.

His post immediately garnered massive amounts of attention, creating widespread buzz and a wave of animated discussions across the Web. The immense tide of support that emerged showed that his set of mockups and ideas for a new way of publishing online had legs. John decided to take the leap, and, together with long-time friend and lead developer Hannah Wolfe, he began working on the preliminary stages of Ghost in earnest.

After six months of hard work, the world got its first sneak peek at Ghost when the Kickstarter campaign to fund its ongoing development was launched. Initially, the goal was to raise £25,000 — equivalent to around $39,000 USD. The campaign surpassed that amount within twelve hours and went on to raise over $300,000 USD while also drawing excited commentary from prominent authorities within the business and web world such as Forbes, Wired, and TechCrunch. In the process, it also secured investments from heavy hitters such as Microsoft, Envato, and WooThemes.

The first public release of Ghost (version 0.3.1) occurred in September 2013. It has been continually evolving since then with an exciting roadmap of new features scheduled for release all the way through to version 1.0, which is tentatively due in early 2015.

Though still in its infancy, Ghost has set out to tackle two major tasks, both of which it has already positioned itself well to achieve. One is a goal most of us are familiar with from the overall way Ghost describes itself as a platform; the other is one perhaps not yet as widely known.

The first of these goals, as you'll see on the @TryGhost Twitter profile, is to initiate *A movement to revolutionize the world of online publishing*. Ghost has brought together the insights of seasoned bloggers and experts in cutting edge web technology in order to reimagine the user experience for content publishers. Ghost sees a world in which there are no technical speed bumps for bloggers, allowing them to put all of their focus and energy into the one thing they really want to do: publish content.

In line with this philosophy, Ghost has replaced the bells and whistles of typical publishing platforms with shortcuts and other simplifications geared towards ease of use. It aims to set itself into the background of the user's attention, instead bringing the content they are working on into the fore. It's named "Ghost" for a very good reason: it sees that its job is being done well if it is little more than an opaque specter that is hardly visible as bloggers go about their business.

The second goal, though not something Ghost explicitly sets out to do at its inception, is to usher in a new wave of support for JavaScript-powered web applications built on Node.js. It's very likely that Ghost will act as a driving force that helps take us from the age of PHP (the dominant language of web platforms) to a new paradigm of lightning fast JavaScript and Node.js-driven apps. Just as WordPress propelled the uptake of PHP in its early days, so too may Ghost propel the uptake of Node.js and JavaScript-powered web development.

JavaScript- and Node.js-based apps have been building in popularity in the technical world for some time due to the plethora of advantages they bring, not least of which is speed. Many people consider that PHP is on the downward slope of its dominance while Node.js continues to be one of the fastest growing platforms online. Additionally, we are seeing more and more technologies making a general shift of focus towards JavaScript. Even WordPress, arguably the biggest PHP project there is, has been gradually rolling out increasing numbers of JavaScript-driven features. All things point to JavaScript and Node.js as being the way of the future.

Until now, the relative newness of Node.js-based technology has meant the average blogger or website builder has not been able to partake in these advantages. Arguably, the major roadblocks to enabling people to access the perks of Node.js apps have been the limited availability of hosting and the technical expertise required. Ghost has shaken that stagnation up thoroughly.

The sudden demand for Ghost support has reached the ears of many hosts. In just a few short months, we have seen new automated Ghost installers pop up, hosts that previously didn't support Node.js setting up services to make Ghost installation easy, and brand new hosts specializing purely in Ghost have also emerged. These developments have opened previously non-existent doors to the very latest and most powerful technologies in a way that's accessible to any user no matter what their level of experience.

Ghost is arguably the first in this new generation of web technology to reach widespread public consciousness, bringing with it a wave of new possibility. If web applications of the past could be paralleled with dial-up internet, then we might draw the comparison that Ghost aims to be lightning fast broadband. Where other platforms may grow to accommodate a myriad of use cases, Ghost sets out to remain focused on doing a single job cleanly and efficiently.

This book is designed to show you exactly how to get started with Ghost. You'll learn everything there is to know about using Ghost from working with the admin interface to creating content. You'll get the information you need to choose the right *automated Ghost install* equipped hosting for your needs. You'll be guided through the more technical processes of manual installation on self-managed servers and local environments. And you'll learn how to design and code your own Ghost themes from scratch, whether for your personal use or to sell in the Ghost marketplace.

By the end of this book, you'll be ready to jump head first into the exciting new world of Ghost!

What this book covers

Chapter 1, The First Steps with Ghost, starts with a tour of Ghost as a blogging platform, Ghost's official hosting platform, and shows you how to use it.

Chapter 2, Manual Installation and Configuration of Ghost, helps you install Ghost locally to develop themes for it. We're going to show you how to do this, and also how to manually install Ghost on a VPS host, as well as discuss the main configuration considerations when hosting your blog.

Chapter 3, Preparing for Theme Development, deep dives into some of the main components you'll want to edit, and setting up your development environment.

Chapter 4, Beginning Ghost Theme Development, helps us set up a template shell for the theme, which is the first step to designing a theme. We'll take a look at all the aspects of a Ghost blog that can be redesigned, and how to prepare your theme shell for them.

Chapter 5, Applying Design Choices and Visual Styling, helps you learn how to apply visual styling and design attractive, responsive Ghost blogs.

Appendix, Markdown Syntax and Ghost Shortcut Keys, contains the list of keyboard shortcuts in Ghost.

What you need for this book

To host a Ghost blog, you need to choose a hosting platform: either based on your own hardware, renting a virtual private server, or via a dedicated Ghost hosting service.

To install manually, you need a computer with Node.js installed using either Windows, Mac OS X, or Linux (Ubuntu and CentOS are demonstrated).

To theme, you can work in any text editor of your choice, though Sublime Text is used throughout the book.

Who this book is for

This book is for anyone looking to start using Ghost. You may have web design experience, or you may be a first time blogger looking to install and theme your very first Ghost blog. Either way, you will learn how to install Ghost on a variety of platforms, and learn how to customize its visual appearance.

Conventions

In this book, you will find a number of styles of text that distinguish between different kinds of information. Here are some examples of these styles, and an explanation of their meaning.

Code words in text, database table names, folder names, filenames, file extensions, pathnames, dummy URLs, user input, and Twitter handles are shown as follows: "For reference, you can see a sample config.js file in the .zip file that came with this book."

A block of code is set as follows:

```
server {
    listen 80;
    listen 443 ssl;
    server_name <your domain name>.com www.<your domain name>.com;
    ssl_certificate         /etc/nginx/ssl/<your domain name>/<your
domain name>.com.crt;
    ssl_certificate_key     /etc/nginx/ssl/<your domain name>/<your
domain name>.com.pem;

    location / {
        proxy_set_header X-Forwarded-For $proxy_add_x_forwarded_for;
        proxy_set_header Host $http_host;
        proxy_set_header X-Forwarded-Proto $scheme;
        proxy_pass          http://127.0.0.1:2368;
    }
}
```

Any command-line input or output is written as follows:

```
cd path/to/ghost/folder
mkdir temp
cd temp/
wget https://ghost.org/zip/ghost-latest.zip
unzip ghost-latest.zip
cd ..
sudo cp temp/*.md temp/*.js temp/*.json .
sudo sudo rm -R core
sudo cp -R temp/core .
sudo cp -R temp/content/themes/casper content/themes

sudo npm install --production
sudo rm -R temp
```

New terms and **important words** are shown in bold. Words that you see on the screen, in menus or dialog boxes for example, appear in the text like this: "Both the settings can be accessed via the **Settings** tab in the top admin menu."

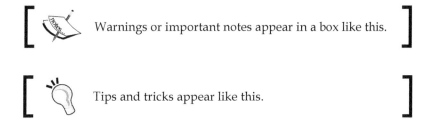

Warnings or important notes appear in a box like this.

Tips and tricks appear like this.

Reader feedback

Feedback from our readers is always welcome. Let us know what you think about this book—what you liked or may have disliked. Reader feedback is important for us to develop titles that you really get the most out of.

To send us general feedback, simply send an e-mail to feedback@packtpub.com, and mention the book title via the subject of your message.

If there is a topic that you have expertise in and you are interested in either writing or contributing to a book, see our author guide on www.packtpub.com/authors.

Customer support

Now that you are the proud owner of a Packt book, we have a number of things to help you to get the most from your purchase.

Downloading the example code

You can download the example code files for all Packt books you have purchased from your account at `http://www.packtpub.com`. If you purchased this book elsewhere, you can visit `http://www.packtpub.com/support` and register to have the files e-mailed directly to you.

Errata

Although we have taken every care to ensure the accuracy of our content, mistakes do happen. If you find a mistake in one of our books—maybe a mistake in the text or the code—we would be grateful if you would report this to us. By doing so, you can save other readers from frustration and help us improve subsequent versions of this book. If you find any errata, please report them by visiting `http://www.packtpub.com/submit-errata`, selecting your book, clicking on the **erratasubmissionform** link, and entering the details of your errata. Once your errata are verified, your submission will be accepted and the errata will be uploaded on our website, or added to any list of existing errata, under the Errata section of that title.

To view the previously submitted errata, go to `https://www.packtpub.com/books/content/support` and enter the name of the book in the search field. The required information will appear under the **Errata** section.

Piracy

Piracy of copyright material on the Internet is an ongoing problem across all media. At Packt, we take the protection of our copyright and licenses very seriously. If you come across any illegal copies of our works, in any form, on the Internet, please provide us with the location address or website name immediately so that we can pursue a remedy.

Please contact us at `copyright@packtpub.com` with a link to the suspected pirated material.

We appreciate your help in protecting our authors, and our ability to bring you valuable content.

Questions

You can contact us at `questions@packtpub.com` if you are having a problem with any aspect of the book, and we will do our best to address it.

The First Steps with Ghost

1

The first thing you'll need to do to get started with Ghost is to set up a brand new blog.

When Ghost was first privately released to its Kickstarter backers, it was something of an arduous process to get the ball rolling, which was to be expected in the very early stages of such a brand new platform. However, it has not taken long for brilliant minds to put themselves to the task of making this process straightforward.

In this chapter, you'll learn about the following topics:

- Ghost's official hosting
- The basic use of Ghost, including what to do immediately after installation and how to navigate within the admin interface
- The essentials of post management in Ghost, including an introduction to Markdown syntax

Automated installation of Ghost

In this section, we're going to assume that you just want a Ghost blog—and you want one fast. We'll show you how to set up the blog on Ghost's official service, Ghost(Pro).

Despite only having been out for a relatively short time, Ghost already has a number of cost-effective hosting options that make installation easy. Ghost's own official hosting service is one of them and so that's what we'll look at in this chapter, but for those who want to explore other options, refer to *Chapter 2, Manual Installation and Configuration of Ghost*.

 If you're interested in more advanced endeavors that require extensive control over servers, or you want local installation for development needs, check out *Chapter 2, Manual Installation and Configuration of Ghost*, where we step you through manual installation processes for both online and local environments.

A background on Ghost's hosting

Before we describe the specifics of Ghost's hosting service, a little background is relevant on how the company itself has set themselves up as an entity and the license they've adopted for the software. This information may well play a part in how you decide which host to use.

Firstly, Ghost is set up as a not-for-profit organization. This means that while staff can receive a wage, every single cent of profit they generate goes straight back into continuing to make Ghost bigger, stronger, and better. Thanks to this structure, there will never be any commercial interests that could lead Ghost astray in the way that often occurs when a company is beholden to shareholders. Nor is Ghost at the risk of being acquired by another entity who may want to change the principles and direction of the project. They have committed themselves to keeping Ghost's priorities in the right place by adopting a legal structure that supports the health of Ghost itself ahead of any individuals involved within it.

Secondly, they have adopted the MIT license rather than any other open source license because they believe it allows for the maximum level of freedom for users and developers. They want people to be able to do anything at all with Ghost and that includes the choice to apply whatever license they may wish to the Ghost-related works they create.

In a nutshell, the team at Ghost is doing everything they can think of to make the future of the platform vibrant, open, and strong.

Part of making that happen is embarking on what they have referred to as a *Sustainable Open Source* approach. Too often, open source projects that have much to offer fall by the wayside due to a lack of funding or are forced to change their model in order to stay afloat. From the outset, Ghost has sought to ensure it continues to remain viable via its own dedicated hosting service. Should you choose to host with Ghost directly, you can be sure the money you put in will go straight towards keeping the project strong.

Using Ghost's hosting solution

On the technical front, probably the biggest advantage of hosting directly with Ghost is that you gain access to their updates as they are released and their team manages all of the backend server security. Ghost and server updates are handled automatically in the background, so you never have to think about them. The second big advantage is that no one knows the software quite as well as the creators themselves, so you're in safe hands.

Ghost(Pro) does not allow backend access to your files, but is rather designed to offer the most streamlined service. This means that if you want to set any customized configurations, or make any major changes on the backend, you will not be able to. This is usually not a problem, because most users just want a reliable platform to host their blog, without too much extra customization. As you grow in confidence with managing your Ghost blog, you may choose a different hosting option, allowing you to tinker with code and use custom settings. *Chapter 2, Manual Installation and Configuration of Ghost*, will help you along if you decide to delve deeper!

Ghost(Pro) also provides the ability to point your own domain, or subdomain, at your Ghost blog. Full instructions on how to go about that can be found at `https://ghost.org/blogs/domains/#setup`, when logged into Ghost.org.

Adding a custom theme only requires going to the Settings section of your My Blogs dashboard, browsing for a theme ZIP file on your computer, and then saving your settings. The theme will then be applied to your blog automatically with no further steps needed.

Pricing to host on Ghost(Pro) starts at $10 per month for a single blog with up to 25,000 views/month. All the plans are monthly plans with no long-term commitments necessary.

For Ghost's full pricing chart visit `https://ghost.org/pricing/`.

And to register a new account at Ghost.org go to `https://ghost.org/`.

Creating a blog on Ghost(Pro)

The Ghost hosting interface is deliberately simple, ensuring there are no confusing options to slow down your installation. Setup is as easy as hitting the **New Blog** button, filling in your preferred blog title, and clicking on the **Create New Blog** button. That's it!

Creating your user account

As soon as you have installed Ghost online, there is one thing that you must do immediately and without delay: register your blog's owner user account.

With Ghost(Pro), you have an overall account you log into at `http://ghost.org`; however, you'll also need a user account for each Ghost blog you create in order to log into their individual admin areas.

Some hosts will take care of this user account setup as part of the installation process, but most will not.

The minute you have finished your installation, you should go to: `http://<yourdomain.ghost.io>/ghost/signup/`, which will look something like the following screenshot:

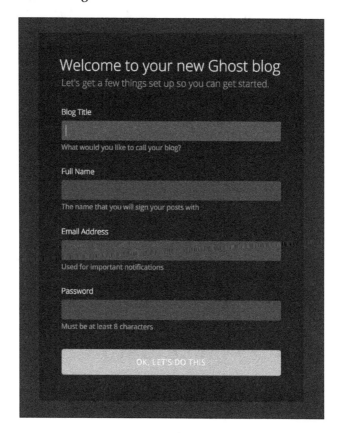

Once there, fill in your name, e-mail address, and password and then click on **SIGN UP** to create your user account.

You must complete this step immediately because until you do that, the form will be open for anyone to come along and create a user account.

Now that your account is created, go ahead and log in.

Configure settings

After you've logged into your account, you're ready to configure some basic settings. The available settings are very simple, so there's not a lot you'll need to do at this stage.

Ghost currently has two settings areas: **General** and **User**. Both the settings can be accessed via the **Settings** tab in the top admin menu. The panels are both fairly self-explanatory, so this will be a brief overview to point out the various features.

General settings

Let's first have a look at the general settings:

The general settings are as follows:

- **Blog Title**: This will be used by most themes in the header as well as sometimes in the footer. Ghost will also output your **Blog Title** in your site's `<title>` tags.

- **Blog Description**: This will also tend to appear in the header of most themes. Ghost will output your **Blog Description** in the description metatag of your site.

- **Blog Logo**: The blog logo is typically positioned in the header or the top of the sidebar in most themes. To add a custom logo, click on the green **Upload Image** button next to the **Blog Logo** label.

- **Blog Cover**: Not all themes use the blog cover image, but those that do, tend to use it as a background for large headers or as the background for the entire site. To add a custom block cover image, click on the green **Upload Image** button next to the **Blog Cover** label.

- **Email Address**: This is the e-mail address to which you'll receive admin-related notifications.

- **Posts per page**: This can be set to determine how many posts a user can see before needing to click through to the next page. This affects post listings on the home page and on tag pages.

- **Dated permalinks**: If checked, this option will add the date of publishing to post permalinks in the `<yourdomain>.com/YYYY/MM/DD/post-title/` format.

- **Theme**: This option will allow you to choose from any themes that were in your blog's `content/themes` directory when it was last started up. Note that new themes uploaded to this directory won't be seen until Ghost is restarted.

 This area is not available on Ghost(Pro), where themes are added via the **Settings** section for each blog instead.

After making any changes to these settings, click on the blue **Save** button in the top-right corner of the screen.

User settings

This section has two main purposes. One is to give you the ability to change your password; you'll see the fields that allow you to do so at the bottom of the page. The other is to enter information that your theme can display in the author profile area on single posts of your blog.

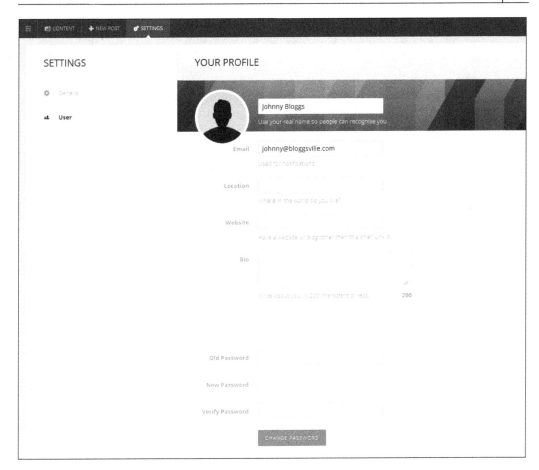

The author profile settings are as follows.

- **Author Image**: In the little circle at the top-left of the user settings, you'll see the author image. To add your own, click on this circle and an uploading window will appear.

- **Author Cover**: This is an image similar to the **Blog Cover** image that can be used by the theme on single posts. It would seem likely that this image may be designed to appear on author profile pages once their functionality is included in Ghost. Click on the **Change Cover** button in the bottom-right corner of the cover image preview to change it.

- **Author Name**: Fill in the name here that you'd like to have displayed publicly as the author of your posts.

- **Email**: This is a required field; however, it can use a different e-mail address than your main admin e-mail. Be aware that this address may be displayed in your author profile on some themes.

- **Location**: Again, the location you enter here will appear in your author profile area should you want people to know where you live. If not, leave this blank.

- **Website**: Add the URL of any other website of yours you'd like people to know about. Most themes will include a hyperlinked display of this URL in the author section of your single posts.

- **Bio**: Include up to 200 characters about yourself to have included in your single post author section.

Content management

The post management process in Ghost is very smooth and simple. In this section, we'll cover the essentials of post management, as well as a couple of features you might need a little more help finding than others.

The content management area

The first page you'll be presented with each time you log in to Ghost is your content management area, which can also be reached anytime by clicking on the **Content** tab in the admin menu. This is where we'll begin looking at how to manage your content. The content management area screen can be seen in the following screenshot:

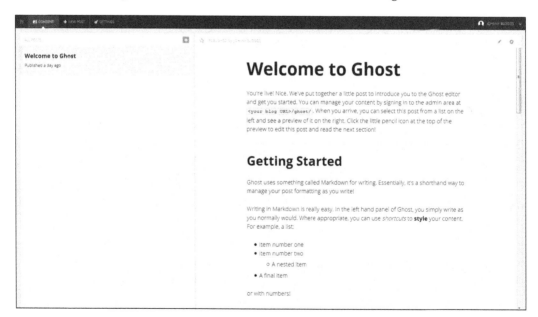

Down the left-hand side you'll see a list of all the content that has been added to your blog so far. On a new site, this content is always the default "Welcome to Ghost" post.

On the right you'll see a preview of whichever post is currently selected from that list.

Creating and deleting posts

To create a new post click on either the **New Post** tab in the admin menu, or the small green plus sign above the post list (highlighted in the following screenshot):

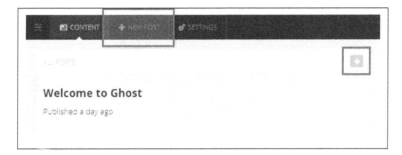

To delete a post, first select it from the list from the left-hand side panel by clicking on its title. Then click on the small grey gear icon in the top right of the post preview and click on **Delete This Post** at the bottom of the menu that pops up.

Converting a post to a page

By default, when you create a new piece of content, it will be generated as a *post*, which means it will appear with all your other posts on your front page. However, you also have the option to convert a post into a *static page*. This will remove the item from your regular list of posts so that it can act as a standalone item, such as an *About Us* page, for example. This makes the page accessible via its URL, but is not a part of the regular post feed. Note that Ghost's navigation menu creation UI is not yet released, so until it has released, any links to static pages have to be hardcoded into a theme, which many themes have done.

Additionally, if the theme has any special formatting in place for the appearance of pages, it will be activated. How this presentation differs will depend on the theme you are using.

To convert a post into a page, click on the same gear item you would when deleting a post and then check the **Static Page** box. Ghost will detect that the box has been checked and automatically convert the post to a page.

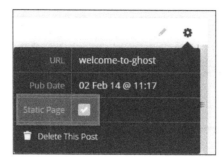

Modifying the permalink or publishing date

When a new post is saved, it has a permalink automatically generated and applied, and when published the publish date is applied. You can change both of these after the fact if you would like. To do so, click on the little gear icon above the post preview, and then click in either of the fields displaying your permalink or date. Enter your new permalink (or URL) or date, ensuring that you maintain the same formatting that was already there, that is, with use of hyphens, spaces, date presentation, and so on. Ghost will detect any changes to these fields and automatically save them.

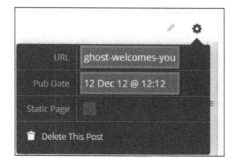

Featured posts

It's also possible to set specific posts to the **Featured** status. This adds a .featured class to the post that a theme may use to style featured posts in a different way, and also makes it possible for a theme to separate them into their own display area. (How this is done will be covered in *Chapter 5, Applying Design Choices and Visual Styling*).

To set a post to the **Featured** status, click on the grey outlined star in the top left of the post preview. When the status is successfully changed to **Featured**, the star will be filled in grey.

Editing existing posts

After you create a new post via the method described earlier, you'll be taken directly into it to begin editing. If you wish to edit an existing post, select it by clicking on its title in the left-hand pane list, and then click on the small grey pencil icon or click on the **Edit This Post** button that appears above its preview. Then perform the following steps:

1. Click on the title to select it.

2. Click on the pencil icon to edit.

The post editing area and inline preview

Once you initiate editing, you'll be taken to the post editing interface. It's here that you'll spend the bulk of your time in Ghost. The post editing screen is shown in the following screenshot:

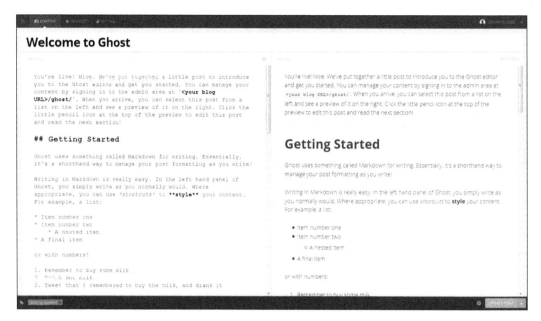

Ghost displays the actual editing space on the left-hand side of the screen. This is where you'll type in your content. To the right, you'll see a real-time preview of your content. As you scroll up or down in your editing space, the preview on the right will automatically scroll to the same position, making it very easy to visualize your content as your blog readers will see it.

At the moment, the content preview uses a default set of styles to determine its appearance. In the future, styles will be drawn from the active theme, so the preview looks exactly as the post will when published.

Setting the title

The large field you see spanning the top of the post editing interface is the post's title. When you first create a new post, the title will not yet be set and you will see this:

To set a new title, or edit an existing one, simply type whatever you wish into this field.

Saving a draft

One of the first things you will want to do, typically as soon as you've typed in your new post's title, is save your draft. To do this, click on the blue **Save Draft** button in the bottom-right of the screen. You can also use *Ctrl + S*.

Adding tags

To add tags to your post, locate and click on the small grey tag in the bottom-left corner of the interface. A cursor will appear and you can type in the tag you wish to apply.

When you have finished typing the tag name, press Enter and your text will be converted into a tag as shown in the following screenshot:

You can repeat this as many times as you wish. The tags that are applied to your post will appear in the single post view and, as of Ghost 0.5.0, each tag will have its own archive page.

The word count display

As you're working on your post, you'll see a very handy live word count tally helping you keep track of your progress. Keep an eye out for this at the top-right corner of your post preview:

Publishing and unpublishing posts

When you're ready to publish your post, hover your mouse over the little downwards pointing arrow on the right end of the **Save Draft** button and you'll see it spin around and point upwards. Click on it and the following menu will appear:

Click on **PUBLISH NOW** and the menu will close, converting the previously blue button into a red one reading **PUBLISH NOW**:

Click on this red button and your post will be published live on the frontend of your blog.

After you have done this, the button will be converted again, back to its former blue color and now reading UPDATE POST:

If you make any edits after publishing, just click on this button to push them to your live post.

Should you need to unpublish the post, the process is essentially the same as for publishing the post. Again, click on the small arrow to the right of what is now the **UPDATE POST** button and the following menu will pop up:

This time select **UNPUBLISH** and the button will turn red, now displaying **UNPUBLISH**:

Click on the red button and your post will no longer be publicly visible while the button will return to its original blue **SAVE DRAFT** state.

Converting a post to page, plus permalink and date modification from the post editor

The functions described earlier that allow you to modify your post's permalink and date, or convert it into a page from the content management area, are also available in the post editing area. They work in the same way as described earlier, the only difference being the location of the little gear icon you need to click on to commence the process. In this case, look for the gear icon to the left of the **SAVE DRAFT / UPDATE POST** button in the bottom-right of the screen.

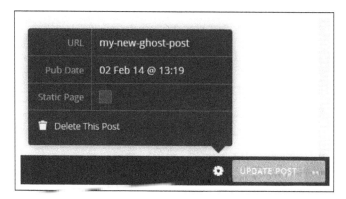

Markdown, image upload, and inline HTML

Now that you know everything there is to know about using Ghost's interface for content management, you're ready to dig into the actual process of writing the content itself.

The fundamental principle behind the writing process in Ghost is that users should be able to blog away without interruption or distraction, with little to no pauses required to click on buttons or do anything other than focus on what they are writing. To that end, one of the major features of Ghost is the Markdown syntax it uses to facilitate post formatting.

Markdown is a system of basic symbols that can be used directly inline with content in order to generate the most common formatting requirements, such as headings, and to handle common tasks such as inserting images.

For example, on most writing platforms, should you wish to format a line of text as *Heading 1*, you would first need to stop writing, take your hand off the keyboard, grab your mouse, highlight the line, and then click on the platform's **H1** button.

But with Ghost, none of this is necessary. You simply enter a single # character at the start of your line and it will present as H1 text.

This means no pauses to take your hands off the keyboard and work with the mouse or interface buttons. Everything becomes a part of a smooth typing process.

At first glance, this may not seem like a huge time saver in itself; however, in application, doing almost everything via the keyboard, without having to pause and mentally change gears to use the mouse, means that you will be able to maintain much greater focus on your writing. Hence, the overall time you save will amount to much more than just the time no longer spent using the mouse.

This example from the Ghost homepage shows just how easy it is to generate some of the most common formatting requirements using Markdown:

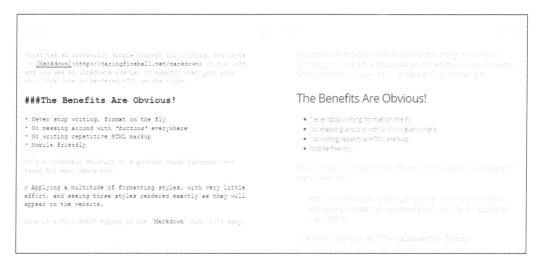

Using Markdown, you can perform the following actions in your Ghost posts:

- Bold text
- Italicize text
- Format text as inline code

- Create text strikethroughs
- Add links
- Insert images
- Create bulleted and numbered lists
- Add blockquotes
- Format text as headings 1 through to 6

For a full breakdown of Ghost Markdown syntax and the keyboard shortcuts you can use to make insertions even faster, please refer to *Appendix*, *Markdown Syntax and Ghost Shortcut Keys*.

To learn more about Markdown visit `http://daringfireball.net/projects/markdown/`.

Image upload

Inserting images is one of the few things you'll use the mouse for when creating Ghost content. The good news is the process is cleverly structured ensuring you don't have to break your writing process to do so until the end.

When you first insert your image markdown, by either pressing Ctrl + Shift + I or typing `![alt](http://)`, a placeholder image will be added into your post preview, as shown in the following screenshot:

When you know you want an image at a certain position in your post, you can go ahead and add a placeholder then continue on with your writing without a pause in your flow. Then after you're finished writing, you can come back and add images to your post.

This process of adding images where placeholders are positioned is also very easy, with two methods to choose from. You can either click on the placeholder image and have it open up a window where you can browse for your image file, or you can drag-and-drop a file directly onto the placeholder to upload.

Inline HTML

On top of its ease of use, one of the beauties of a Markdown-based post editor is you can also place raw HTML straight into your post and it won't be stripped out. If there's something you need to do in your post that doesn't have associated Markdown syntax, you can just add in the code you need directly.

One of the best applications of this is the insertion of videos. You don't need any plugins or an extra functionality to place videos from the most common sites into your post. Just copy the iframe embed code they provide you, such as the type you would get from YouTube, for example, and paste it straight into your post.

Hosting Ghost on other providers

There's a huge array of different third-party providers of Ghost installations. VPS hosting is one popular option. The two VPS providers we are going to cover are DigitalOcean and Amazon EC2. Both of these providers have a one-click installation of Ghost, so you still do not need to worry about manually installing Ghost. The manual installation will be covered in the next chapter though.

While we are only covering two VPS providers, there are many other places you can host Ghost. A great place to go for more information is a website that we created called `www.howtoinstallghost.com`. We have many instructions on many different providers, so feel free to check out that site if you are looking to host elsewhere.

DigitalOcean

DigitalOcean is a **Virtual Private Server** (**VPS**) hosting company with a one-click Ghost installation. They have taken the code provided by the Ghost team and integrated it with their own hosting platform. DigitalOcean runs all of their website hosting on Solid State Drives, which helps make the VPS servers run even faster and decrease your page load times. The greatest benefit of hosting on DigitalOcean is that not only is your Ghost blog live almost immediately, but you also get full access to the server on which it runs.

What this means is that you can access the server and make any changes you want. For instance, if you would like to host a second Ghost website on your server, you have the power to do that. Likewise, if you want to make special configurations or update to their latest nightly version of the code, you can do that as well. While it is not necessary for you to access the server to run your Ghost blog, having the ability to do so is a useful feature. With DigitalOcean, you have to update to the new Ghost software manually, but this should be very easy going forward.

DigitalOcean has played a big part in the Ghost community, even before Ghost was released to the public. The fact that they have an instant install of Ghost, as well as allow their users to have backend access to the server, makes them an outstanding option to host your Ghost blog. DigitalOcean is actually the company that we use to host all of our blogs.

The way DigitalOcean works as a service in general is to provide what they call "droplets". Droplets operate as self-contained servers, which means that they give you control over everything from your choice of operating system, for example Ubuntu and CentOS, to security, which coding languages are supported, and so on. When you purchase a new droplet, everything is installed fresh from the operating system and up. The process of installing Ghost on DigitalOcean is fairly simple, but we have created a step-by-step guide that you can find at `http://www.howtoinstallghost.com/how-to-install-ghost-on-digital-ocean-vps/`.

You can get a DigitalOcean VPS with Ghost and one terabyte of traffic for $5 a month.

The **Ghost** image from Digital Ocean will set your new droplet up with Ubuntu 12.04 as an operating system, with Ghost preinstalled and ready to go. After registering and creating a new droplet, you'll have the choice to select an image under **Applications**. Choose the **Ghost on x.x.x 14.04** image and the setup will be handled for you. You'll be able to access your blog immediately via the IP address allocated to you by DigitalOcean.

You should be prepared for the fact that setting up a custom domain name to point at your site and handling updates is a little more involved as you'll need to work with command line via an SSH client such as Putty (http://www.putty.org).

 If command-line server management is something you're already comfortable with or intend to learn, there is assistance available via the following tutorial written by Ghost's own lead developer Hannah Wolfe at https://www.digitalocean.com/community/articles/how-to-use-the-digitalocean-ghost-application.

Amazon EC2

Amazon offers a cloud hosting service called EC2. With EC2, anyone can launch a cloud-based server. The best part is that, with a new Amazon AWS account, you can host what they call a "Micro" instance, which allows you to run Ghost, free of charge for one year.

EC2 has a marketplace where individuals and companies upload pre-made images of software for users to launch and use for themselves. If you visit the marketplace and search for Ghost, you will see that there are already images ready to use. This makes installing Ghost extremely simple. All you need to do is launch your own instance of the image and Amazon will provide a URL to visit, and your Ghost blog is up and running.

As EC2 is a virtual server, you have backend access to your Ghost blog. This allows you to make any changes on the backend that you would like; however, because the image you used already has Ghost installed and running, you do not need to access the backend if you so choose.

The only downside with using EC2 is that as Ghost and other server software do not update automatically; you are responsible to make updates as needed.

Because the microtier is free, Amazon EC2 is a great way to try out Ghost. EC2 has been an extremely popular way for people to host their Ghost blog, and there is no reason not to try it out.

 We maintain an image of Ghost to facilitate the automated installation of it, to offer an easy place to try out Ghost for free. There's more information and instructions at http://www.howtoinstallghost.com/how-to-setup-an-amazon-ec2-instance-to-host-ghost-for-free/.

Summary

That's it. You've just taken your first steps with Ghost!

You now have all the information you need to choose the host that best suits your needs. You know what to do immediately after installation and can navigate Ghost's admin interface. You can configure your Ghost settings, manage your content, and work with the post editor. You should also have a basic grasp on the concept of the Markdown syntax.

If you've made your decision, and want to go with Ghost(Pro), and now want to customize your Ghost blog's look and feel, you will also need to install a copy of Ghost on your computer, ready for theme development. Head to the next chapter where we cover how to install Ghost locally.

2
Manual Installation and Configuration of Ghost

In this chapter, we will discuss how to install Ghost manually on your computer or a VPS. Given installing on a VPS requires many of the same steps as a local installation, you'll also see what additional steps you need to take to install Ghost manually on a VPS, based on the two most popular operating systems VPS hosts tend to run: Ubuntu and CentOS.

If you are new to using the command line, you may want to look at one of the automated installs instead of installing manually, because it can get a little tricky. We are going to give you all the commands you will need, but it may get complicated for someone who has never used the tools before.

This chapter covers the following topics:

- Manually installing Ghost
  - Using the command line and SSH
  - CentOS (local and VPS)
  - Ubuntu (local and VPS)
  - OSX (local)
  - Windows (local)

- Additional configuration
  - Pointing a custom domain to your blog
  - Hosting multiple blogs on a single VPS
  - Keeping Ghost running on a VPS
  - Upgrading Ghost

- Troubleshooting and finding help

Manually installing Ghost on your local computer

In this section, we will detail how to install Ghost locally on your personal computer and on your web hosting company's server. We will be covering Ubuntu, CentOS, Mac OS X, and Windows. The steps to install Ghost are largely the same whether installing locally on your personal computer or on a remote server. However, there are some key differences that we will highlight.

Command-line interface and SSH access

In order to install Ghost manually, a command-line tool and, if you are using a VPS, an application for **Secure Shell (SSH)** access is needed. If you are using Mac OS X or Linux, you can use the Terminal application. On Mac OS X, it is located in your **Applications | Utilities** folder. For Windows, you need to download an application in order to use SSH; however, if you're installing locally, you can use the command prompt by navigating to **Accessories | Command Prompt**. For SSH access, we suggest using Putty (http://www.putty.org/).

The majority of steps will be performed using the command line, and we provide the exact command that needs to be executed. Occasionally, you will need to type in part of a command. For example:

```
tar -xzf node-latest.tar.gz
cd [name of expanded node directory]
```

In the first command, when we expand node-latest.tar.gz, the name of the folder that will be created is unknown, but in our case, it is called node-v0.10.25. Therefore, our change directory command would look like this:

```
cd node-v0.10.25/
```

You can see an example of this in the following screenshot:

```
● ○ ○                    Desktop — bash — 80×24
Ghosts-Mac:desktop ghost$ curl -O http://nodejs.org/dist/node-latest.tar.gz
  % Total    % Received % Xferd  Average Speed   Time    Time     Time  Current
                                 Dload  Upload   Total   Spent    Left  Speed
100 13.0M  100 13.0M    0     0  2633k      0  0:00:05  0:00:05 --:--:-- 2843k
Ghosts-Mac:desktop ghost$ tar -xzf node-latest.tar.gz
Ghosts-Mac:desktop ghost$ ls
node-latest.tar.gz      node-v0.10.25
Ghosts-Mac:desktop ghost$ cd node-v0.10.25/
```

For those new to using command-line interface, it's beyond the scope of this book to fully explore command-line operations—though we'll be demonstrating all the commands you need to execute specific steps throughout. If you want to learn more about this, see the following link (don't be put off by the title! It's a great way for beginners to learn how to leverage the power of the command line):

http://cli.learncodethehardway.org/book/

Identifying your VPS operating system

If you have a VPS but are unsure what operating system is installed, you can SSH into your VPS, and run uname -a to determine if it is Ubuntu or CentOS, as shown in the following example:

```
ghost@192.168.0.13:~# uname -a
Linux 192.168.0.13 3.2.0-54-virtual #82-Ubuntu SMP Tue Sep 10 20:31:18
UTC 2013 x86_64 x86_64 x86_64 GNU/Linux
```

On Ubuntu, running uname -a will output something similar to the one shown in the following screenshot:

```
root@ip-172-31-15-194:~# uname -a
Linux ip-172-31-15-194 3.2.0-54-virtual #82-Ubuntu SMP Tue Sep 10 20:31:18 UTC 2013 x86_64 x86_64 x86_64 GNU/Linux
root@ip-172-31-15-194:~#
```

On CentOS, the output will look like this:

```
ghost@192.168.0.13 [~]# uname -a
Linux server 2.6.32-358.18.1.el6.x86_64 #1 SMP Wed Aug 28 17:19:38 UTC
2013 x86_64 x86_64 x86_64 GNU/Linux
```

Here's the screenshot as well:

```
-bash-4.1# uname -a
Linux ip-172-31-13-25 2.6.32-279.22.1.el6.x86_64 #1 SMP Wed Feb 6 03:10:46 UTC 2013 x86_64 x86_64 x86_64 GNU/Linux
-bash-4.1#
```

Installing Ghost on Ubuntu (VPS and local)

We need to perform the following steps to install Ghost on Ubuntu OS. These steps will work on all versions of Ubuntu 12.04 and higher:

1. First, make sure your Ubuntu operating system is up to date:

    ```
    sudo apt-get update
    sudo apt-get upgrade
    ```

2. Next, install the tools needed to compile Node.js:

    ```
    sudo apt-get install build-essential zip
    ```

3. Download and install Node.js:

    ```
    cd /tmp/
    wget http://nodejs.org/dist/node-latest.tar.gz
    tar -xzf node-latest.tar.gz
    cd [name of expanded node directory]
    ./configure
    make
    sudo make install
    ```

4. Create a Ghost user:

    ```
    sudo adduser ghost
    ```

5. Download and install Ghost:

    ```
    sudo mkdir -p /var/www/
    cd /var/www/
    sudo wget https://ghost.org/zip/ghost-latest.zip
    sudo unzip -d ghost ghost-latest.zip
    sudo chown -R ghost:ghost /var/www/ghost/
    sudo rm ghost-latest.zip
    ```

6. Switch to the ghost user:

    ```
    su - ghost
    ```

7. Install Ghost:

```
cd /var/www/ghost
npm install --production
```

8. Configure Ghost (skip this step if installing locally):

```
vi config.example.js
```

9. In the **Production** section, change `host: '127.0.0.1'`, to:

```
host: '0.0.0.0',
```

10. Save and exit

11. To start Ghost, run:

```
npm start --production
```

After running the command in step 11, you should see an output that says **Ghost is running...**. You're now running Ghost!

```
○ ○ ○        .ssh — ghost@ip-10-179-49-107:/var/www/ghost — ssh — 84×9
[ghost@ip-10-179-49-107 ghost]$ npm start --production

> ghost@0.4.1 start /var/www/ghost
> node index

Ghost is running...
Your blog is now available on http://my-ghost-blog.com
Ctrl+C to shut down
```

This means that Ghost has started successfully and you can now browse to your Ghost website. If you installed Ghost locally and did not edit the `config.js` file, type the `127.0.0.1:2368` URL into your browser, and you will see your Ghost blog. If you edited your `config.js` file, head to the URL or the IP address where Ghost is set up to run it.

Now that you see your Ghost home page, add `/ghost/` to the end of the URL to create your Ghost admin user (for example, `127.0.0.1:2368/ghost/` or `<yourdomain>.com/ghost/`).

If you run into any errors with starting up Ghost, see our *Troubleshooting* section at the end of this chapter.

Configuring Ghost on Ubuntu for VPS

We will be using Nginx, a popular web server software, to run on port 80, which will then proxy requests to port 2368, the port that Ghost will be running on. This section assumes that you have already purchased a domain name from a registrar such as NameCheap and have configured the domain to point to your VPS. If you need assistance setting up your domain name, we would recommend contacting your domain registrar and they will assist with the configuration. To configure Ghost on Ubuntu, perform the following steps:

1. Install Nginx:

   ```
   sudo apt-get install nginx
   ```

2. Configure Nginx to proxy all requests to port 80 to `localhost:2368` by placing the following configuration in `/etc/nginx/conf.d/ghost.conf`:

   ```
   server {
     listen 80;
     server_name example.com;

     location / {
       proxy_set_header    X-Real-IP  $remote_addr;
       proxy_set_header    Host       $http_host;
       proxy_pass          http://127.0.0.1:2368;
     }
   }
   ```

3. Restart Nginx to load the new configuration:

   ```
   sudo service nginx restart
   ```

Installing Ghost on CentOS (VPS and local)

Perform the following steps:

1. Update your operating system:

   ```
   sudo yum update
   ```

2. Install the additional packages that are needed to compile Node.js:

   ```
   sudo yum groupinstall development
   ```

3. Download and install Node.js:

```
cd /tmp/
curl -O http://nodejs.org/dist/node-latest.tar.gz
tar -xzf node-latest.tar.gz
cd [name of expanded node directory]
./configure
make
sudo make install
```

4. Create a Ghost user:

```
sudo useradd ghost
```

5. Download and install Ghost:

```
sudo mkdir -p /var/www/
cd /var/www/
curl -L -O https://ghost.org/zip/ghost-latest.zip
unzip -d ghost ghost-latest.zip
sudo chown -R ghost:ghost /var/www/ghost/
sudo rm ghost-latest.zip
```

6. Switch to the Ghost user:

```
su - ghost
```

7. Install Ghost:

```
cd /var/www/ghost/
npm install --production
```

8. Configure Ghost (skip this step if installing locally):

```
vi config.example.js
```

9. In the **Production** section, change host: '127.0.0.1', to:

```
host: '0.0.0.0',
```

10. Save and exit

11. To start Ghost, run:

```
npm start --production
```

After running the command in step 11, you should see an output that says **Ghost is running...**. You're now running Ghost!

```
● ○ ○        .ssh — ghost@ip-10-179-49-107:/var/www/ghost — ssh — 84×9
[ghost@ip-10-179-49-107 ghost]$ npm start --production

> ghost@0.4.1 start /var/www/ghost
> node index

Ghost is running...
Your blog is now available on http://my-ghost-blog.com
Ctrl+C to shut down
```

This means that Ghost has started successfully and you can now browse to the Ghost website. If you installed Ghost locally and did not edit the config.js file, type the URL 127.0.0.1:2368 into your browser, and you will see your Ghost blog. If you did edit your config.js file, head to the URL or IP address where Ghost is set up to run.

Now that you see your Ghost home page, add /ghost/ to the end of the URL to create your Ghost user (for example, 127.0.0.1:2368/ghost/ or example.com/ghost/).

If you run into any errors with starting up Ghost, see our *Troubleshooting* section at the end of this chapter.

Configuring Ghost on CentOS for VPS

We will be using Nginx, a popular web server software, to run on port 80, which will then proxy requests to port 2368, the port that Ghost will be running on. This section assumes you have already purchased a domain name from a registrar such as NameCheap and have configured the domain to point to your VPS. If you need assistance setting up your domain name, we would recommend contacting your domain registrar and they will assist with the configuration.

1. Install Nginx:

   ```
   sudo yum install nginx
   ```

2. Configure Nginx to proxy all requests to port 80 to localhost 2368 by placing the following configuration in /etc/nginx/conf.d/ghost.conf:

   ```
   server {
     listen 80;
     server_name example.com;

     location / {
       proxy_set_header   X-Real-IP $remote_addr;
   ```

```
        proxy_set_header   Host    $http_host;
        proxy_pass      http://127.0.0.1:2368;
    }
}
```

3. Restart Nginx to load the new configuration:

```
sudo service nginx restart
```

Installing Ghost on Mac OS X (local)

We need to perform the following steps to install Ghost on Mac OS X:

1. Update your operating system by clicking on the apple in the upper-left-hand corner and clicking on **Software Update**.

2. Go to http://nodejs.org/download/ and download the .pkg Macintosh Installer. Double-click on the file that was downloaded and go through the installation process, selecting all of the default values.

3. Execute the following commands on the command line in the Terminal app (located in /Applications/Utilities):

```
mkdir -p ~/ghost
cd ~/ghost
curl -L -O https://ghost.org/zip/ghost-latest.zip
unzip ghost-latest.zip
rm ghost-latest.zip
npm install --production
```

Configuring Ghost on OS X

To configure Ghost on OS X, perform the following steps:

1. We are going to be making changes to the Ghost configuration file. If you just plan to host Ghost locally on your own computer and do not want to allow access from anywhere else, you can skip this step. If you are installing Ghost on a remote server or want to allow access beyond your personal computer, this step is necessary.

    To make the configuration file, we're going to use the vi text editor. For a list of vi commands visit http://www.lagmonster.org/docs/vi.html.

```
cp config.example.js config.js
vi config.js
```

2. In the **Production** section, note the following sections:

```
url: 'http://my-ghost-blog.com',
and
host: '127.0.0.1',
port: '2368'
```

3. Replace the preceding code with the following one:

```
url: '[your Ghost URL or IP]',
and
host: '0.0.0.0',
port: '80'
```

 Check the example `config.js` in the ZIP file that came with this book to see what it should look like if you are unsure what to change.

4. To start Ghost run:

```
npm start --production
```

After running the command in step 4, you should see an output that says **Ghost is running....** You're now running Ghost on OS X!

```
● ○ ○     .ssh — ghost@ip-10-179-49-107:/var/www/ghost — ssh — 84×9
[ghost@ip-10-179-49-107 ghost]$ npm start --production

> ghost@0.4.1 start /var/www/ghost
> node index

Ghost is running...
Your blog is now available on http://my-ghost-blog.com
Ctrl+C to shut down
```

This means that Ghost has started successfully and you can now browse to the Ghost website. If you installed Ghost locally and did not edit the `config.js` file, type the `127.0.0.1:2368` URL into your browser, and you will see your Ghost blog. If you edited your `config.js` file, head to the URL or IP address where Ghost is set up to run it.

Now that you see your Ghost home page, add /ghost/ to the end of the URL to create your Ghost user (for example, 127.0.0.1:2368/ghost/ or <yourdomain>.com/ghost/).

If you run into any errors with starting up Ghost, see the *Troubleshooting* section at the end of this chapter.

Installing Ghost on Windows (local)

To install Ghost on a Windows OS, we need to perform the following steps:

1. Update your operating system by navigating to **Control Panel | System** and **Security | Windows Update | Check for updates**.

2. Go to http://nodejs.org/download/ and click on the Windows Installer to download the .msi installer. Once the download has completed, run the installer, selecting all of the default values.

3. Now go to the http://ghost.org, log in, and click on the blue **Download Ghost Source Code** button.

4. In the location of your choice, create a folder called Ghost and expand the contents of the ghost.zip file into it.

5. Now, open the Node.js command prompt, which can be found in your **Start** menu. (There is a Node.js app and a Node.js command prompt. Make sure you open the command prompt.)

6. Change the directory to the Ghost folder you created:

   ```
   cd [ path to where you have created the Ghost folder ]
   ```

7. Now install Ghost:

   ```
   npm install --production
   ```

Configuring Ghost on Windows

To configure Ghost, perform the following steps:

1. We are going to be making changes to the Ghost configuration file. If you just plan to host Ghost locally on your own computer and do not need to allow access from anywhere else, you can skip this step. If you are installing Ghost on a remote server or want to allow access beyond that computer, this step is necessary.

2. Inside the `Ghost` folder, there is a file called `config.example.js`. Open this file in any text editor and change the following sections:

    `url: 'http://my-ghost-blog.com',`

    and

    `host: '127.0.0.1',`

    `port: '2368'`

    to:

    `url: '[your Ghost URL or IP]',`

    and

    `host: '0.0.0.0',`

    `port: '80'`

3. Save this file as `config.js` and exit the text editor.

> Check the example `config.js` in the `.zip` file that came with this book to see what it should look like if you are unsure what to change.

4. Now, to start Ghost run:

    `npm start --production`

After running the command in step 4, you should see an output that says **Ghost is running...**.

```
express@3.4.6 node_modules\express
├── methods@0.1.0
├── cookie-signature@1.0.1
├── fresh@0.2.0
├── range-parser@0.0.4
├── debug@0.7.4
├── buffer-crc32@0.2.1
├── cookie@0.1.0
├── mkdirp@0.3.5
├── send@0.1.4 (mime@1.2.11)
├── commander@1.3.2 (keypress@0.1.0)
├── connect@2.11.2 (uid2@0.0.3, pause@0.0.1, qs@0.6.5, raw-body@1.1.2, bytes@0.2
.1, negotiator@0.3.0, multiparty@2.2.0)

mysql@2.0.0-alpha7 node_modules\mysql
├── require-all@0.0.3
├── bignumber.js@1.0.1

C:\Users\Ghost\Desktop\ghost>npm start --production

> ghost@0.4.0 start C:\Users\Ghost\Desktop\ghost
> node index

Ghost is running...
Your blog is now available on http://my-ghost-blog.com
Ctrl+C to shut down
```

This means that Ghost has started successfully and you can now browse to the Ghost website. If you installed Ghost locally and did not edit the `config.js` file, type the `127.0.0.1:2368` URL into your browser, and you will see your Ghost blog. If you edited your `config.js` file, head to the URL or IP address where Ghost is set up to run it.

Now that you see your Ghost home page, add `/ghost/` to the end of the URL to create your Ghost user (for example, `127.0.0.1:2368/ghost/` or `example.com/ghost/`).

If you run into any errors with starting up Ghost, refer to the *Troubleshooting* section at the end of this chapter.

Additional configuration for VPS usage

There's a few additional configuration steps to consider when hosting your blog on a VPS.

Pointing a custom domain at Ghost (VPS)

Now that your have Ghost up and running, a common next step will be pointing a domain name at your blog. This section will cover the concepts of pointing your custom domain name at the server hosting Ghost. These steps will be specific for a domain purchased at Namecheap to a DigitalOcean droplet running Ghost. We have chosen to document NameCheap and DigitalOcean because of their popularity, but almost every domain name registrar has similar steps.

 If you run into any problems, contact your domain name registrar, they make these changes for people all the time.

Perform the following steps to point your custom domain to Ghost:

1. Buy a domain name at Namecheap.
2. Now you need to configure your domain to point to DigitalOcean. To do that click on the **My Account** tab in Namecheap and then on **Manage Domains**.
3. Next click on your domain name.
4. On this page click on **Transfer DNS to Webhost**. Then you have the option to input custom DNS Servers. By inputting the custom DNS server, you can configure where your domain name points to. In this example, you can input the nameservers for DigitalOcean.

5. In custom DNS servers 1 to 3, fill in the following details:

   `ns1.digitalocean.com`

   `ns2.digitalocean.com`

   `ns3.digitalocean.com`

6. Now click on **Save Changes**.

7. Next log in to your DigitalOcean account. Once logged in, click on the DNS link.

8. Click on the **Add Domain** button in the upper-right corner.

9. Now, select your Ghost droplet name and fill in your domain name.

Hosting multiple Ghost blogs on the same VPS

If you are using a VPS and would like to host multiple Ghost blogs on that VPS, we have provided some configurations to help you. We have an example configuration for Nginx as it is recommended for Ghost.

 Your Ghost instances must each be running on a separate port. This change can be made in the `config.js` file in the Ghost folder.

Nginx

On both CentOS and Ubuntu, the configuration files can be found in `/etc/nginx/`.

```
server {
  listen 80;
  server_name blog-one.com;

  location / {
    proxy_set_header    X-Real-IP $remote_addr;
    proxy_set_header    Host        $http_host;
    proxy_pass          http://127.0.0.1:2368;
  }
}

server {
  listen 80;
  server_name blog-two.com;

  location / {
    proxy_set_header    X-Real-IP $remote_addr;
```

```
    proxy_set_header    Host    . $http_host;
    proxy_pass          http://127.0.0.1:8080;
  }
}
```

Keeping Ghost running (VPS)

In all of the manual walkthroughs in this chapter, the last command is:

`npm start --production`

This command will start Ghost and keep it running while your current terminal session remains open. This is fine when testing or checking out Ghost for the first time, but is not a feasible option if you are looking to keep your Ghost blog up and running. The problem with `npm start` is that it will only continue to run as long as you have the connection established. This means that if you close your command prompt, your Ghost blog will quit running. Therefore, a process manager is needed to keep Ghost up and running at all times in the background.

The forever process manager

`forever` is a process manager that performs very well with Ghost. It will start Ghost and restart Ghost if it crashes. `forever` works great on CentOS and Ubuntu.

The following steps should be performed while Ghost is not running and should be executed from the Ghost user that was created during the steps in the *Installing Ghost on CentOS (VPS and local)* and *Installing Ghost on Ubuntu (VPS and local)* sections:

1. Change to your Ghost user:

    `su - ghost`

2. Before installing `forever`, you must be inside the Ghost directory:

    `cd /var/www/ghost`

3. Install `forever`:

    `npm install forever`

4. Add the new `forever` command to your path:

    `echo "export PATH=/var/www/ghost/node_modules/forever/bin:$PATH" >> ~/.bashrc`

    `. ~/.bashrc`

5. Start Ghost with `forever`:

    ```
    NODE_ENV=production /var/www/ghost/node_modules/forever/bin/
    forever start index.js
    ```

You should see the **Forever processing file: index.js** message.

```
  winston@0.7.2 (cycle@1.0.3, stack-trace@0.0.7, eyes@0.1.8, async@0.2.10, req
uest@2.16.6)
Ghosts-Mac:ghost ghost$ sudo NODE_ENV=production forever start index.js
warn:    --minUptime not set. Defaulting to: 1000ms
warn:    --spinSleepTime not set. Your script will exit if it does not stay up f
or at least 1000ms
info:    Forever processing file: index.js
Ghosts-Mac:ghost ghost$
```

At this point, `forever` should have started Ghost. You are free to continue using your command prompt without interrupting Ghost. You can check to make sure that forever has started Ghost by using the `sudo forever list` command or by browsing to your site to see if it is up and running. Here are some of the most useful forever commands:

- `forever stopall`: This stops all the processes of `forever`
- `forever restartall`: This restarts all the processes of `forever`
- `forever logs`: This shows the logs of all the current `forever` processes
- `forever list`: This shows a list of all the `forever` processes

> For more information on `forever`, check out their Github page at `https://github.com/nodejitsu/forever`.

Adding SSL for security

If you are going to be using Ghost in production, it is a good idea to protect your login page with an SSL certificate. If your login page is not protected with SSL, your administrator password will be sent across your network in plain text making it easy to steal if someone is snooping on your network. To add SSL for security, perform the following steps:

1. The first step is to get an SSL certificate. There are many different SSL certificate providers out there, so choose the one you trust or ask your hosting provider how to get one and follow their instructions to obtain your certificate.

2. Now that we have created and received the SSL certificate files, we want to copy those files into a Nginx SSL directory:

```
mkdir /etc/nginx/ssl

cp server.crt /etc/nginx/ssl/server.crt

cp server.key /etc/nginx/ssl/server.key
```

3. After those two files are in place, we need to make some changes to the Nginx config. Go ahead and open up your Ghost Nginx `conf` file:

```
sudo vi /etc/nginx/sites-available/ghost.conf
```

4. You do have to add a few lines so that Nginx knows where the SSL certificate is. Here is an example configuration; make sure you change the domain name in this configuration to your web address:

```
server {
    listen 80;
    listen 443 ssl;
    server_name <your domain name>.com www.<your domain name>.com;
    ssl_certificate          /etc/nginx/ssl/<your domain name>/<your
domain name>.com.crt;
    ssl_certificate_key      /etc/nginx/ssl/<your domain name>/<your
domain name>.com.pem;

    location / {
        proxy_set_header X-Forwarded-For $proxy_add_x_forwarded_
for;
        proxy_set_header Host $http_host;
        proxy_set_header X-Forwarded-Proto $scheme;
        proxy_pass         http://127.0.0.1:2368;
    }
}
```

5. Save and exit the `conf` file and restart Nginx:

```
sudo service nginx restart
```

6. Nginx should be all set up now. The last change we need to make is inside of the actual Ghost `config.js` file. So, let's open up that file:

```
sudo vi /var/www/ghost/config.js
```

7. Once you have opened the file, scroll down to the **Production** section. Under the URL line create a new line and add the following:

```
forceAdminSSL: true,
```

8. Save and exit.

9. Restart Ghost.

Once you have restarted Ghost, you should only be able to log into Ghost over HTTPS. This is highly recommended as it will help to keep your blog more secure.

Upgrading Ghost

At regular intervals, Ghost monitors for new releases. When the Ghost team releases a new version, you will see a notification like the following screenshot.

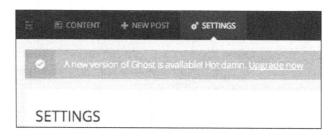

Clicking on the **Upgrade now** link will take you to `http://ghost.org/download` so you can download the latest release.

Whether you installed Ghost locally, or on a remote server, you can use the following steps to upgrade your Ghost installation (note that in a future release of Ghost the upgrade process will be built into Ghost and can be completed with a one-click process):

1. Stop Ghost. If you are using `forever`, change to your Ghost user and run:

    ```
    forever stopall
    ```

2. Download and move updated files into place:

    ```
    cd path/to/ghost/folder
    mkdir temp
    cd temp/
    wget https://ghost.org/zip/ghost-latest.zip
    unzip ghost-latest.zip
    cd ..
    sudo cp temp/*.md temp/*.js temp/*.json .
    sudo sudo rm -R core
    sudo cp -R temp/core .
    sudo cp -R temp/content/themes/casper content/themes

    sudo npm install --production
    sudo rm -R temp
    ```

All of the updated files have been placed and Ghost is ready to be started. If you are developing locally, you can use the `npm start --production` command to start Ghost; or if you are running Ghost on a VPS, you can start Ghost with the following forever command:

```
cd /var/www/ghost
NODE_ENV=production /var/www/ghost/node_modules/forever/bin/forever start index.js
```

Troubleshooting

Even with detailed installation instructions, problems may still arise while installing or starting Ghost. We will look at some of the common errors that occur.

listen EADDRINUSE IN USE

If you come across this error when trying to start Ghost, this means that the port on which you are trying to start Ghost is already in use. This error usually occurs when trying to start Ghost, but another website or application is already running on this port. Usually this happens when someone tries to start Ghost but it is already running. In this instance, you will either need to stop the application or start Ghost on a different port. If you choose to start Ghost on a different port, this change should be made in the `config.js` file.

listen EADDRNOTAVAIL

When starting Ghost, if you see this error, it means that something is wrong in the `host:` or `port:` section of your `config.js` file. Usually this is caused by a syntax error, or by entering an address or port that does not exist. Here is the syntax that should be used in the `config.js` file:

```
host: '127.0.0.1',
port: '2368'
```

For reference, you can see a sample `config.js` file in the `.zip` file that came with this book.

Command not found

This error typically happens when you try to use `sudo`. This error can happen when you use the `npm` or `forever` commands. The reason you get this error is because the `sudo` user issuing the command does not know the location of the application. In order to get the commands to work, you need to use the full file path to the application. The commands should look something like this:

```
sudo /usr/local/bin/npm start index.js
```

The preceding command uses the full filepath to `npm`, unlike `sudo npm start index.js`.

Places to find help

If you have any trouble installing and running Ghost, there are many resources that can help. The first, and most popular place, is the official Ghost forum at (`https://ghost.org/forum/`). The Ghost forum has a great community and people are always willing to help.

Ghost also has an official IRC channel (`irc.freenode.net`, `#Ghost`) with quite a few regular users. The IRC is a good place if you are looking for immediate answers to a problem.

> Two of this book's authors, Andy and David also run a few websites: Ghost For Beginners (`http://ghostforbeginners.com`), All About Ghost (`http://allaboutghost.com`), and How to Install Ghost (`http://howtoinstallghost.com`). We feel they are also a great resource if you are looking for more detailed install instructions or articles relating to other Ghost features. If you have any questions, feel free to comment on either site and we will answer as best as we can.

Summary

Throughout this chapter, we have covered how to install Ghost on four of the main operating systems as well as some of the more common errors. We have also shown you how to keep Ghost running with forever process manager. If you followed the mentioned steps, your Ghost blog should now be up and running. Congratulations on successfully installing Ghost! The next chapter will cover the inner workings of Ghost and Handlebars.js, the template languages Ghost uses. This will give you a great baseline on how Ghost works and how to create themes for it.

3
Preparing for Theme Development

In order to get you ready to develop Ghost themes, there are some preliminary steps you'll need to take and some base information you'll need to be aware of. There are four languages we're going to be working with as we walk you through the creation of Ghost themes.

The two primary languages used will be HTML and CSS, as you would expect with any web design process, and we'll also use a small amount of JavaScript in order to enhance responsive functionality and browser compatibility.

HTML and JavaScript will be typed directly into your documents in the regular fashion; however, rather than manually creating raw CSS, we're going to use a CSS preprocessor called *Stylus* to make the development process much easier for you. So you won't be typing up your CSS in raw form, rather you'll be coding in the Stylus syntax, which will be explained in more detail later in this chapter.

The fourth language, although the term *language* is more loosely used in this case, is Handlebars.js, a templating system that acts as the connection between your theme files and Ghost's data.

The chapter assumes you already have a local installation of Ghost, having followed the steps in *Chapter 1*, *The First Steps with Ghost*, or *Chapter 2*, *Manual Installation and Configuration of Ghost*, and that you know how to access a terminal/command window on your computer in order to run commands.

It will also assume that you have a basic level of familiarity with coding for the Web; however, if you don't, you should still be able to follow along just fine by reading closely.

In this chapter, you'll learn about:

- Handlebars.js logic-less templating
- Creating CSS via Stylus
- Setting up a code editor to work with the languages you'll be using
- Setting up a theme development project that handles JavaScript minification and automatic Stylus compilation

Handlebars' logicless templating

The use of Handlebars.js is at the core of how Ghost themes operate. Handlebars is what is known as a "logic-less" templating language, which in a nutshell means its job is simply to display blog-specific content.

When creating themes for Ghost, it is important to understand that the platform keeps a very clear delineation between design, which is the area themes are responsible for, and functionality, which is the area Ghost itself and apps are responsible for. The logic-less nature of Handlebars helps to ensure that Ghost themes don't step outside the role for which they are intended, and that is controlling the presentation of a blog.

Unlike PHP-driven templating systems, Ghost's Handlebars-driven template files don't handle any manipulation of data, custom database queries, or any other processes driven by logic. In a Ghost theme, you can't write functions, create variables, or evaluate conditions outside of checking whether or not there is content available for display.

Handlebars gets its name from its distinctive use of double or triple curly brackets to denote template tags, for example:

```
{{pagination}}
```

All Handlebars template tags are predefined by Ghost, or by apps, so wherever a template tag like the preceding one is placed in your theme, the corresponding predetermined content will be placed on that location. Ghost theme template files primarily comprise these Handlebars template tags in combination with HTML.

The preceding example template tag is the one Ghost has predefined to output pagination on the front page of your blog or your tag archives. So to have pagination appear in your theme, all you need to do is insert this template tag anywhere in the appropriate theme file. Note that we'll cover which template tags you'll need and how they should be used in which parts of your theme later.

There are a few key elements of how Handlebars.js works that you'll find important to be aware of when you get started coding up your theme's template files.

Double and triple curly braces

Template tags can have double curly braces like this:

```
{{date}}
```

Or triple curly braces like this:

```
{{{body}}}
```

The difference is that the first will escape any HTML content that is delivered, while the second won't. What this means is that if there is a string of HTML included in the content pulled in via a template tag, double curly braces will show you the HTML itself on the screen, while the triple curly braces will actually render the HTML into the page.

For that reason, pay close attention to using triple braces where it's indicated they should be, as per the previous example, where the {{{body}}} tag uses three braces. If you see a string of code appearing on your page for no apparent reason, change your double braces to triple braces at the point you see the unwanted display.

Handlebars' paths

Sometimes individual pieces of content can be nested inside a parent content object. For example, in Ghost, all the information saved by navigating to the **Settings** | **User** of the admin panel is available under the author parent content object; however, to access the individual content items you must identify the child item you wish to display via a Handlebars path, expressed as a dot.

To show an image of the author, you would target the author object's image child by separating the two terms with a dot, as follows:

```
{{author.image}}
```

Similarly, you could display the author's bio or website URL:

```
{{author.bio}}
{{author.website}}
```

The each and foreach block helpers

The {{#each}} helper is used to cycle through groups of multiple parent content objects, allowing you to directly access the child items of each. The name of the parent object is included in the opening tag and whatever is included between the each tags will be repeated for every parent object that is cycled through:

```
{{#each parentobject}}
{{childcontent}}
{{/each}}
```

Built into Ghost is a custom version of this helper that is specific to the display of published blog posts. It is used in the same way as an {{#each}} helper, but is written as follows:

```
{{#foreach post}}
{{content}}
{{/foreach}}
```

So for each parent item, that is, each published blog post, whatever is between the foreach tags will be repeated. We use this to display things such as the title, content, and tags for each available post.

The if helper

The default function of the if helper is very simple, which is purely to check if there is any available content to be retrieved via a specific template tag.

For example, before outputting HTML to display an author's location, you can check to see if there is location information available to display:

```
{{#if author.location}}
<p itemscope itemtype="https://schema.org/PostalAddress"><span item
prop="addressLocality">{{author.location}}</span></p>
{{/if}}
```

If you didn't use the preceding check and the user had not saved anything into the location field, an empty paragraph would be displayed. Using this technique, you can make sure that sections of HTML are only output in your theme if there is content to go along with them.

In Ghost themes, the `if` helper has an additional function, in that, it can be used to check on some extra private properties available for some content objects. For example, it can be used to check if a post is the first in the list like this:

```
{{#if @first}}
<div>First post</div>
{{/if}}
```

We'll cover more on the specific properties that can be checked with the `if` helper later on.

The unless and else helpers

The `unless` helper has the inverse functionality of the `if` helper. It checks to see if a certain piece of content is not available before proceeding. This can be used to create fallback content where appropriate.

For example, if the user has not uploaded an image of themselves, you might wish to fall back to a custom avatar image you have designed instead:

```
{{#unless author.image}}
<div id="my_custom_avatar_fallback"></div>
{{/unless}}
```

The `unless` helper can be used by itself; however, you could alternatively create the same functionality described in the above example by using the `else` helper, as long as it's in conjunction with an `if` helper as follows:

```
{{#if author.image}}
<img src="{{author.image}}">
{{else}}
<div id="my_custom_avatar_fallback"></div>
{{/if}}
```

Template tag parameters

In some cases, template tags can accept parameters that will affect how they output content. For example, in Ghost, a blog post's content can be displayed with the basic template tag:

```
{{content}}
```

Alternatively, it can have the number of words to display specified:

```
{{content words="100"}}
```

We'll give a thorough rundown on the template tag parameters available for you to work with in Ghost as part of *Chapter 4, Beginning Ghost Theme Development*.

Comments

If you would like to include comments in your theme, for example, to help users identify areas they might like to edit, use double curly braces with an exclamation mark immediately after the opening two braces:

```
{{! This is how comments are written with Handlebars}}
```

The comment will appear in the template file, but not in the HTML that is output during rendering.

 For more information on handlebars and how they are used in Ghost, check out their documentation page at http://themes.ghost.org/.

Creating CSS via the Stylus preprocessor

Instead of manually typing out each line of CSS you're going to require for your Ghost theme, we're going to get you set up to become highly efficient in your development through use of the CSS preprocessor named *Stylus*.

Stylus can be described as a way of making CSS smart. It gives you the ability to define variables, create blocks of code that can be easily reused, perform mathematical calculations, and more. After Stylus code is written, it is compiled into a regular CSS file that is then linked into your design in the usual fashion.

It is an extremely powerful tool with many capabilities, so we won't go into them all here; however, we will cover some of the essential features that will feature heavily in our theme development process.

Variables

Stylus has the ability to create variables to hold any piece of information, from color codes to numerical values for use in your layout. For example, you could map out the color scheme of your design like this:

```
default_background_color = #F2F2F2
default_foreground_color = #333
default_highlight_color = #77b6f9
```

You could then use these variables all throughout your code instead of having to type them out multiple times:

```
body {
  background-color: default_background_color;
}
a {
  color: default_highlight_color;
}
hr {
  border-color: default_foreground_color;
}
.post {
  border-color: default_highlight_color;
  color: default_foreground_color;
}
```

After the preceding Stylus code was compiled into CSS, it would look like this:

```
body {
  background-color: #F2F2F2;}
a {
  color: #77b6f9;
}
hr {
  border-color: #333;
}
.post {
  border-color: #77b6f9;
  color: #333;
}
```

So not only have you been saved the trouble of typing out these color code values repeatedly, which in a real style sheet means a lot of work, but you can also now easily update the color scheme of your site simply by changing the value of the variables you created.

Variables are very handy for many purposes, as you'll see when we get started on theme creation.

Stylus syntax

Stylus code uses a syntax that reads very much like CSS, but with the ability to take shortcuts in order to code faster and more smoothly. With Stylus, you don't need to include curly braces, colons, or semicolons. Instead, you use tab indentations, spaces, and new lines.

For example, the code used in the last section could actually be written like this in Stylus:

```
body
   background-color default_background_color

a
   color default_highlight_color

hr
   border-color default_foreground_color

.post
   border-color default_highlight_color
   color default_foreground_color
```

You may think at first glance that this code is more difficult to read than regular CSS; however, shortly we'll be getting you running with a syntax highlighting package that will make your code look like this:

```
default_background_color = #F2F2F2
default_foreground_color = #333
default_highlight_color = #77b6f9

body
     background-color default_background_color

a
     color default_highlight_color

hr
     border-color default_foreground_color

.post
     border-color default_highlight_color
     color default_foreground_color
```

With the syntax highlighting package in place you don't need *punctuation* to make your code readable as the colors and emphasis allow you to easily differentiate between one thing and another.

The chances are very high that you'll find coding in this manner much faster and easier than regular CSS syntax. However, if you're not comfortable, you can still choose to include the curly braces, colons, and semicolons you're used to and your code will still compile just fine.

The golden rules of writing in Stylus syntax are as follows:

- After a class, ID, or element declaration, use a new line and then a tab indentation instead of curly braces
- Ensure each line of a style is also subsequently tab indented
- After a property, use a space instead of a colon
- At the end of a line, after a value, use a new line instead of a semicolon

Mixins

Mixins are a very useful way of preventing yourself from having to repeat code, and also to allow you to keep your code well organized and compartmentalized. The best way to understand what a mixin is, is to see one in action. For example, you may want to apply the same font-family, font-weight, and color to each of your heading tags. So instead of writing the same thing out manually for each H tag level, you could create a mixin as follows:

```
header_settings()
  font-family Georgia
  font-weight 700
  color #454545
```

You could then call that mixin into the styles for your heading tags:

```
h1
  header_settings()
  font-size 3em
h2
  header_settings()
  font-size 2.25em
h3
  header_settings()
font-size 1.5em
```

When compiled, you would get the following CSS:

```
h1 {
  font-family: Georgia;
  font-weight: 700;
  color: #454545;
  font-size: 3em;
}

h2 {
  font-family: Georgia;
  font-weight: 700;
  color: #454545;
  font-size: 2.25em;
}
h3 {
  font-family: Georgia;
  font-weight: 700;
  color: #454545;
  font-size: 1.5em;
}
```

As we move through the Ghost theme development process, you'll see just how useful and powerful Stylus is, and you'll never want to go back to handcoding CSS again!

Setting up your environment

You may already have a code editor you prefer to use; however, for the purposes of following along with this book, I strongly recommend you try the setup we're about to describe, whereby you'll have excellent syntax highlighting for both Handlebars and Stylus. If you're firm on not wanting to try a different editor, please try and find a compatible syntax highlight package for each of these languages as it will make reading and editing your code far easier.

Sublime Text 2 and Package Control

The editor we'll be using is the brilliant Sublime Text 2. If you're not already a Sublime Text 2 user, you can download a copy at `http://www.sublimetext.com/2`.

 Sublime Text 3 is available, but for now just grab Version 2 and install it onto your machine.

The next thing you'll need to do is install Package Control for Sublime Text, which we'll be using to pull in your syntax highlighting packages.

The command required to install Package Control changes often with updates to Sublime Text, so unfortunately we can't include it for you here. Please visit `https://sublime.wbond.net/installation#st2` and follow the instructions you find there.

After you have installed Package Control, you're ready to grab your syntax highlighters.

Installing Stylus and highlighting Handlebars syntax

To install the Stylus and Handlebars packages in Sublime Text 2, follow these steps:

1. Navigate to **Preferences** | **Package Control** in the main top menu.

   A menu will appear with a list of options, each prefaced with **Package Control**.

2. Click on the list item titled **Package Control: Install Package**.

   Wait for a little while as the available packages are looked up. You'll then see a list of packages with a search field above them.

3. In the search field, type the name of the package you want to install.

   Search for Stylus to bring up the Stylus highlighting package, named **Stylus**. Search for `Handlebars` to bring up the Handlebars highlighting package, named **Handlebars**.

4. When you see the package you want, come up below the search field, click on the item to install it.

Follow this process once for each of the two packages.

You now have your Sublime Text 2 editor installed along with syntax highlight for all the languages you'll be using (HTML, CSS, and JS are in-built), and so you're almost ready to start coding.

The final step is to take care of creating a project environment that will handle compiling your Stylus code into CSS and minifying your JavaScript, which is what we'll take care of next.

Creating your project environment

Outside of the actual folder that will contain your Ghost theme, we'll also be using a separate folder, one that contains your Stylus code as well as uncompressed JavaScript. We'll be using a JavaScript taskrunner system called *Grunt* to both compile your Stylus from here into a CSS file in your theme, and to minify the little bit of JavaScript we'll be using and write that into your theme folder.

You can think of this folder as the source of your theme, while the theme folder itself will contain the finished product. You might also like to use this folder to hold any PSDs or other source material you utilize in future projects.

This system depends on Node.js to handle the compilation and minification processes; however, as long as you have already followed the instructions in *Chapter 2, Manual Installation and Configuration of Ghost*, and installed Ghost on your computer, you will have installed Node.js as part of the process. That chapter will also have shown you how to run commands via the command window/terminal on your computer, so if you completed that section yet please go ahead and do it now before proceeding.

For this section, you should also download the source files that come along with this book as you'll be provided with a readymade package that will handle most of the project setup process for you.

You will need the zip file named, `ProjectSetup.zip`.

Installing Grunt

With Node.js in place on your machine, the next step is to install Grunt globally on your computer so that it can be accessed from wherever you decide to set up your project folder.

Open up a command window / terminal and type the following command:

```
npm install -g grunt-cli
```

You'll see a series of lines of text in the window while Grunt is being installed. Wait until they finish and the command prompt returns, which means the installation is complete.

Creating a project folder

Create a new folder wherever you'd like on your computer, (though if you installed Ghost at C:\ghost I'd recommend creating this folder at C:\), and give it a name to represent the theme you'll be creating. In this case, we'll keep it generic and go with LearningGhostSource.

Extract the ProjectSetup.zip file you downloaded with the source materials for this book into this folder. It will create the following three folders:

- **stylus**: This will hold your Stylus files, with several .styl files and folders inside that will help you design quickly and easily when following *Chapter 5, Applying Design Choices and Visual Styling*.

- **js**: This will hold your uncompressed JavaScript files, with two files inside named modernizr.js and responsive_iframes.js.

- **compiler**: This contains the scripts that will compile your Stylus and minify your JavaScript.

Installing the project compiler

Now, move into the Compiler folder and open a command window / terminal.

On Windows, I feel the easiest way to open a command window in a particular location is to first go there via **Windows Explorer** then hold *Shift*, right-click and choose **Open command window here**. If you're on Mac or Linux, cd (change directory) to the location manually.

Once you have a command prompt in the Compiler folder, type the following command then press *Enter*:

```
npm install
```

This will fetch the scripts required to handle compilation and minification. As you did when installing Grunt, wait for the lines of text to stop and a new command prompt to appear. When this happens, the installation of the project compiler is complete.

Set project options

The scripts you just installed will handle all your compilation and minification automatically; however, the only thing you need to do is tell it where your installation of Ghost is and what your theme's name is.

From inside the `Compiler` folder, open up the file named `Gruntfile.js`. Find these lines towards the bottom:

```
'ghost_location': '../../ghost/',
'ghost_theme_name': 'LearningGhost',
```

Enter the location of your installation of Ghost (from *Chapter 2, Manual Installation and Configuration of Ghost*) in between the `' '` marks after `'ghost_location':`.

Note that this is a relative path to the location of your `Gruntfile.js` file. Each time you see the `'../'` notation, that means the system will look up one level from where `Gruntfile.js` is.

For example, the default config will work for you if your `Gruntfile.js` file is at `C:\LearningGhostSource\compiler\Gruntfile.js`, and your installation of Ghost is at `C:\ghost`.

Then enter the name of the theme you will be creating in between the `' '` marks after `'ghost_theme_name':`. This will be the theme folder the compiler will look for to write in your CSS and JavaScript files. For the purposes of this exercise, leave it as `'LearningGhost'`.

Run the watch task

Your project folder is now fully installed and ready to watch your source files for changes. To initiate the `watch` task, with your command window / terminal still pointed at your `Compiler` folder, type the following command and then press *Enter*:

```
grunt watch
```

You should then see the following appear:

```
Running "watch" task
Waiting...
```

As long as this `"watch"` task is running, whenever you save any changes to any file in the `stylus` folder with a `.styl` extension, your CSS will be automatically compiled into the appropriate location in your theme.

For now, end the `"watch"` task as we don't yet have your theme created in order to allow files to be written into it. To end the task, press *Ctrl + C*. A message will appear saying:

```
Terminate batch job (Y/N)?
```

Press *Y* and then *Enter* and the `"watch"` task will end. We'll reactivate it again later after we've started creating your theme and are ready to develop its CSS.

Minifying JavaScript

When you want to minify JavaScript, the process will be very similar to the above, in that, you will type this command then press *Enter*:

```
grunt uglify
```

This will combine and minify the files from your `js` folder and write them into your theme. However, we're not ready for this command, so don't run it just yet as we'll be using it later at the appropriate point in the theme development process.

Summary

You now have everything in place and ready to begin your Ghost theme development process.

You understand the essentials of working with Handlebars, the templating language used by Ghost, and Stylus, the means by which we'll be creating your theme's CSS. You have your editor set up with syntax highlighting for all the languages you'll be using. And you have your project folder in place where you'll create your source files, as well as the scripts installed that will compile your Stylus to CSS and minify your JavaScript.

In the next chapter, we begin Ghost theme development, starting with a rundown of the array of design options you currently have to choose from then moving to hashing out your main concept. We'll then create your theme folder structure and start coding up your theme's template files. From there, we'll create the CSS for your theme via Stylus, and generate responsiveness and maximum browser compatibility. Finally, we'll cover the last few steps involved in preparing your theme for deployment.

4
Beginning Ghost Theme Development

This chapter will be a guide to kickstart your first Ghost theme from scratch.

However, we won't be just walking you through designing one or two specific example themes, because then all you would know would be just how to make one or two specific themes. Instead, we're aiming to equip you to build any kind of theme you might want to for Ghost. In order to do this, we're not going to focus directly on design, but rather on all the little tools and tricks available through the Ghost theme API that you currently have to work with as a designer.

First, we'll cover the spaces on a Ghost blog you get to control via a theme design, such as your main index area, your individual posts and so on. We'll refer to each of these as *themeable areas*. Secondly, we'll look at the visual building blocks Ghost currently offers you to put in those areas, that is, items such as blog titles, logos, and post content you can place in your theme.

We'll then go over a summary of the extra tools that Ghost gives you to work with to format theme content differently depending on conditions such as whether a viewer is looking at a featured post, an item with a particular tag, and so on. We'll also cover what Ghost doesn't include at this stage.

From here, you'll plan out your design concept in the easiest possible way by going through a *Quick start theme quiz* where your answers will form the basis of your design.

Once you know how to work with the full range of theming options Ghost gives you, you'll have the knowledge to select from those options and assemble themes in as many different ways as you choose.

Your first step in the actual production of your theme will be to create a theme shell; an unstyled theme with all the essentials in place that you can mold into any type of theme you want. After creating this shell, you'll add test content to your local Ghost installation, activate your new theme and prepare to move onto the next stage.

This chapter includes the following topics:

- The currently available design options in Ghost
  - ° Ghost's themeable areas
  - ° Ghost's theme building blocks
  - ° Extra design tools in Ghost
  - ° What Ghost doesn't include
- Quick start theme quiz
- Creating your theme shell
- Setup file and folder structure
  - ° Running the first CSS and JS compile into theme
  - ° Adding basic code to template files and package.json
- Adding test content and activating your theme

An overview of the currently available design options

We won't get into the technicalities of how to actually code these aspects up right away, but instead just begin with the information you need to hash out your design concept.

Then, after we work through putting together your design concept, we'll get into which files to create and what code to write in order to take that concept into production.

The themeable areas of a Ghost blog

The different themeable areas of Ghost are as follows:

- **Default (required)**: This is a wrapper around all your other theme areas. It typically holds your header, footer, and any other elements that should appear everywhere throughout your theme.

- **Index (required)**: This is a paginated list of your posts beginning on your homepage with the most recent.

- **Post (required)**: Display of an individual post. Posts can be tagged.

- **Tag Archive (optional but recommended)**: This is a list of all posts under a specific selected tag. If no theme styling is included, tag archives will use the code from the `Index` file.

- **Page (optional but recommended)**: This is a display of a static page. If no theme styling is included, pages will display the same way as your *Post* area.

The primary theme design building blocks

With Ghost using Handlebars, many attributes of the blog settings are available, so a theme can pull them dynamically. For example, a blog title is something you can change in your settings, so, instead of then needing to go change the title in your theme, you can use Handlebars attributes so it will update on the blog as well without any change in code.

New attributes are being added constantly to Ghost, but here are some of them along with where they can be used in the themes:

- The following attributes are available everywhere:
  - **Blog title**
  - **Blog description**: Use this as a short tagline or a longer *About* passage.
  - **Blog logo**
  - **Blog cover**: Use as a header background, sidebar background, or overall site background.

- The following attributes are only available in the *Index*, *Post*, and *Tag Archive* areas:
  - **Post titles**
  - **Post content**: HTML included, that is, images, links, and videos. On *Index* and *Tag Archive*, this can be limited to a word or character count.
  - **Post date**: This can show the actual time of publishing, for example, **21st Jan 2014**, or relative time, for example, **1 Month Ago**.

- The following attribute is only available in the *Index*, *Post*, and *Tag Archive* areas:
  - **Post tags**: Each tag displays links to an archive of all posts sharing that tag.

- The following attributes are only available in *Index* and *Tag Archive* areas:
  - ◦ **Post Excerpt**: This is stripped of HTML, text only, limited by word or character count.
  - ◦ **Pagination**: This is the number of posts per round of pagination set under **Settings | General | Posts per page**.

- The following attributes are only available in the *Post* and *Page* areas:
  - ◦ **Author name**
  - ◦ **Author location**
  - ◦ **Author website**
  - ◦ **Author bio**
  - ◦ **Author image**
  - ◦ **Author cover**

- The following attributes are only available in the *Tag Archive* area:
  - ◦ **Tag Archive Name**: This is the name of the tag whose archive is being viewed.

Extra design tools

The extra design tools available are as follows:

- **The `Featured` post status**: When a user sets a post to this status, it will have a class of `featured` added to it, and can be identified with a Handlebars conditional check. This is used to display featured posts before regular posts, and/or to style featured posts in a different way.

- **The `{{#has}}` helper**: This tool checks if any post has (or doesn't have) a particular tag and modifies its display based on the result. This is used to create customized displays for things such as posts tagged as `video`, `image`, `text`, and so on.

- **Content blocks**: They allow elements of the default wrapper to be modified through other themeable areas. For example, on a single post, check for a `video` tag, and if found, alter the layout width to allow for widescreen playback.

- **`@first` and `@last`**: They identify the first and last post in any index or tag archive list. They are used to create enhanced layouts or highlight opening and closing posts.

- `@even` **and** `@odd`: They identify every second post alternately. They are used to zebra stripe.

- `columns`, `@rowStart`, **and** `@rowEnd`: They tell Ghost how many columns are in your layout, will keep track of your posts, and allow you to output which ones are at a row start and which are at a row end.

The current exclusions in Ghost

There are also a few things that are common to other blogging platforms that Ghost doesn't, as of yet, include. Some are planned on the roadmap, some are likely to arrive via apps created by the community, and some are not on the horizon at all.

While these items might appear in the not too distant future, we won't be using them in this theming guide, because even if we did, it would be via incorrect (hackish) methods that would then have to be redone in the future. It's much better to wait until properly crafted updates to Ghost or plugins are released that will handle the job in the correct fashion. The following items are currently excluded by Ghost:

- **Menus**: These are on the roadmap for Ghost core, but not until a few versions down the track. However, it's highly likely a plugin, or several plugins, will be released by the community to handle this shortly after the release of apps.

- **Sidebar Widgets**: Ghost doesn't have a means to drag-and-drop custom content into positions such as sidebars, so you should plan to work with the content items listed previously. However, again it's very likely that apps will appear to handle this type of functionality.

- **Comments**: Ghost has determined (from the outset) that inclusion of a comments system in core was unnecessary given the many quality comments systems available, such as Disqus. It's possible to integrate Disqus into themes via code; however, apps to handle this automatically for users are likely to become available very soon.

Quick start theme quiz

Now that you know what you have available to work with in creating your Ghost theme, you can begin making decisions on how to put the available elements together. You'll find what is essentially a quiz that you can run yourself at the beginning of each new design in this section.

These questions are not intended to give you hard-and-fast rules you must follow, so if you want to do something not covered here, by all means, feel free. But as you kick off your learning process, they will give you a simple method to make commencing a new design much easier.

If you have an idea in your mind already, you can go through and answer the questions in a way that fits what you're imagining. And if you don't have any ideas yet, you can just decide on your answers as you go along then when you'll have the basis of your design in place, ready for the next section.

Default

Let us have a look at the default features first:

Questions	Answers
Overall layout; single or twin column?	**Single column**: header area (holding blog title, description, logo) stacked on top of posts area and footer
	Twin column: sidebar area (holding blog title, description, logo) positioned next to posts area and footer
Use the blog cover image?	Don't use
	Use as site background
	Use as header background if single column / sidebar background if twin column
If single column layout: header height; full, large or auto?	**Full**: before the user scrolls down, set header area to full height of screen to create whole page blog cover
	Large: set the header to be large, but not the full height of the screen
	Auto-fit header height only to content the header contains (blog title, description, logo)

Index and tag archive

Let us have a look at the quiz for index and tag archive:

Question	Answers
Posts; excerpt, full or trimmed?	Excerpt: HTML stripped, text only, trimmed to max words/characters
	Full content: HTML included, entire post
	Trimmed content: HTML included, trimmed to max words/characters
If excerpt: show post's first image/video/soundcloud?	Show
	Don't show

Question	Answers
Zebra stripe (alternate colors every second post)?	Zebra stripe
	Don't zebra stripe
Featured posts; list first above default posts?	Yes
	No
Featured posts; style differently to default posts?	Yes
	No
Specifically tagged posts; style differently for certain tags, for example, video, music, and so on?	Yes: if so, list which tags you want to look different to others and in what way; for example, make a wider space for video playback or allocate different background colors.
	No

Tag archive

The following table will guide you for quizzing the tag archive:

Question	Answers
Style the whole tag archive page differently for specific tags?	Yes: if so, list which tags you want to look different to others and in what way, for example, create a grid/gallery out of all image tagged posts.
	No

Post and page

Let us now quiz for post and page:

Question	Answers
If single column layout AND header height full/large: post header style?	Auto-height with blog cover as background
	Auto-height without blog cover as background

Post

For the post feature, we'll look into the following questions:

Question	Answers
Should a featured single post be styled differently from a default single post?	Yes
	No
Should a specifically tagged single post be styled differently for certain tags?	Yes: if so, as in the previous section list, which tags you want to look different to others and in what way.
	No

In the next section, we'll show you how to implement the decisions you made for the preceding questions. This will give you the means to mix and match in any way you please.

From there, you can add your own unique styling over the top, and you'll be able to create a virtually unlimited number of different themes!

Creating your theme shell

The very first thing we're going to do is set up a basic theme shell, without any styling applied to it, that you can use as the foundation of this theme and any other you build after it.

The setup file and folder structure

We'll begin by getting the file and folder structure of your theme set up inside your local offline Ghost installation.

Go to `content/themes` in your local installation and create a new folder for your theme. As we mentioned in *Chapter 3, Preparing for Theme Development*, we'll name it `LearningGhost`.

Inside that folder, create five new files. The templates your Ghost theme will use are as follows:

- `default.hbs`
- `index.hbs`
- `post.hbs`
- `tag.hbs`
- `page.hbs`

As you can see, the names of these template files correspond with the themeable areas talked about previously, with each one being responsible for the presentation of each of these areas.

Note that it's also possible to include an error.hbs file which allows you to create your own page for 400 and 500 errors. However, Ghost provides quite a nice looking error page by default, so we won't be making a customized version in this guide.

Additionally, create a sixth file inside the LearningGhost folder named package.json.

This is the file you'll enter your theme's proper name and version number into, so it will show up for users when selecting themes via the admin panel. In future, this file will also allow you to specify other assets that your theme depends on, such as Ghost plugins, so they can be automatically installed along with your theme.

As well as the files listed above, your theme will also contain assets such as CSS, JavaScript, font files, and images. In order for Ghost's {{assets}} helper (which we'll be using) to find these files, they must be contained inside a folder named assets.

First, create a new folder within your LearningGhost theme folder and name it assets. Within the assets folder, create an additional four folders named:

- css
- fonts
- images
- js

When you're done, your new theme folder should look like this:

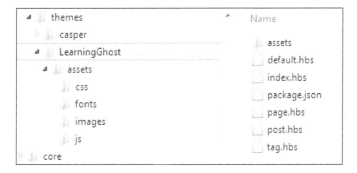

Running the first CSS and JS compile into theme

Now that you have your theme structure in place, it's time to run the first compile from the `LearningGhostSource` project folder you created in the *Creating a project folder* section of *Chapter 3, Preparing for Theme Development*.

Open up a command window/terminal at `LearningGhostSource\compiler` and run the following command:

`grunt stylus`

This command compiles all the files in the `LearningGhostSource\stylus` folder into your theme to give you a basic style sheet.

If you look at `assets\css` inside theme, you should now see a file named `screen.css` in there. This file contains the essential basis for your theme's styles, including a version of `Normalize.css`, typography settings, and a few other basics.

Now, in the same location, run the following command:

`grunt uglify`

This takes the two files in `LearningGhostSource\js`, combines them, minifies them, and writes a file into your theme.

In `assets\js`, you should now see a file named `all.min.js`.

One part of what this combined file does is to load `Modernizr.js`, which will help to ensure that the current standard code is understood by out-of-date browsers. The other part is a custom script that ensures videos, soundcloud embeds, and anything else entered via an iframe will resize responsively in your theme.

Adding basic code to template files and package.json

Using Sublime Text, as per the info in *Chapter 3, Preparing for Theme Development*, open up each of the files mentioned in the upcoming sections.

package.json

Enter the following code into this file:

```
{
  "name": "Learning Ghost",
  "version": "0.1.0"
}
```

Simply enter the name of your theme next to the `name` parameter, and the version number of your theme next to the `version` option.

This file will require more information in the future, but for the time being this is all that's required.

default.hbs

Enter the following code into this file:

```
<!DOCTYPE html>
<html>
<head>
    {{! Document Settings }}
    <meta charset="UTF-8" />
    <meta http-equiv="X-UA-Compatible" content="IE=edge" />

    {{! Page Meta }}
    <title>{{meta_title}}</title>
    <meta name="description" content="{{meta_description}}" />

    <meta name="HandheldFriendly" content="True" />
    <meta name="viewport" content="width=device-width, initial-
scale=1.0" />

    <link rel="shortcut icon" href="{{asset "favicon.ico"}}">

    {{! Styles'n'Scripts }}
    <link href='//fonts.googleapis.com/css?family=Open+Sans:400,700,40
0italic,700italic' rel='stylesheet' type='text/css'>
    <link rel="stylesheet" type="text/css" href="{{asset "css/screen.
css"}}" />
    <script type="text/javascript" src="{{asset "js/all.min.js"}}"></
script>

    {{! Ghost outputs important style and meta data with this tag }}
    {{ghost_head}}
```

```
</head>
<body class="{{body_class}}">

    {{! Document header }}
    <header class="blog_header_lg" role='banner' itemscope
itemtype='http://schema.org/WPHeader'>

        {{#if @blog.logo}}<a href="{{@blog.url}}"><img src="{{@blog.
logo}}" alt="{{@blog.title}}" /></a>{{/if}}
        <h1 class="blog_title_lg"><a title="{{@blog.title}}" href='{{@
blog.url}}'>{{{@blog.title}}}</a></h1>
        <p class="blog_description_lg"><a title="{{@blog.title}}"
href='{{@blog.url}}'>{{{@blog.description}}}</a></p>

    </header>

    {{! Document main }}
    <main class="posts_area_lg">{{{body}}}</main>

    {{! Document footer }}
    <footer class="blog_footer_lg" itemscope itemtype='https://schema.
org/WPFooter'>

        <p><a class="subscribe icon-feed" href="{{@blog.url}}/
rss/">Subscribe!</a></p>
        <p>All content copyright <a href="{{@blog.url}}">{{{@blog.
title}}}</a> &copy; 2013 &bull; All rights reserved.</p>
        <p>Proudly published with <a class="icon-ghost" href="http://
tryghost.org">Ghost</a></p>

    </footer>

    {{! Ghost outputs important scripts and data with this tag }}
    {{ghost_foot}}
    <script language="javascript" type="text/javascript">responsive_
iframes();</script>

</body>
</html>
```

This is the code that will wrap every page of your theme by default. Let's take a quick look at some of the Ghost-specific things being done here.

The wrapper code and {{{body}}} tag

First, we have the essential HTML5 `html`, `head`, and `body` tags. Rather than having this type of code in separate files loaded at the beginning and end of other templates, as you might in WordPress for example, this is all handled in a single file.

This is done by placing the `{{{body}}}` tag where you want the other template files of your theme to load. Note the triple curly braces to prevent HTML escaping as mentioned in *Chapter 3, Preparing for Theme Development*.

The meta content

Note the `{{meta_title}}` and `{{meta_description}}` tags used in the head section. These generate meta tag output dynamically depending on where the visitor is on the site.

The {{asset}} tag

The `style.css` and `all.min.js` files we just generated are loaded into the theme via the `{{asset}}` tag, for example, `{{asset "css/screen.css"}}`. This ensures Ghost always finds theme assets, and that they can be cached.

This tag is also used to load the default favicon: `{{asset "favicon.ico"}}`.

The {{ghost_head}} tag

This tag is essential and must always be included right before the end of the head section.

The {{body_class}} tag

This tag outputs different classes depending on where the user is on the site.

Document <header> section and {{blog}} object

In this section, we are loading the blog's logo, title, and description, each linked to the blog's main URL, so the content in the header acts as the home button. The `@blog` object contains all four of these pieces of data via Handlebars paths/dot notation, as well as any blog cover image, which we will discuss further in a later section:

- `{{@blog.logo}}`: This outputs the blog logo image URL
- `{{{@blog.title}}}`: This outputs the blog title string

 Use triple curly braces to allow users to include HTML such as `<em>` or `<br />`.

- {{{@blog.description}}}: This outputs the blog description string

 Use triple curly braces to allow users to include HTML such as <em> or

- {{@blog.url}}: This outputs the blog root URL
- {{@blog.cover}}: This outputs the blog cover image URL

Note this is a header in the HTML5 sense, that is, it contains header data relative to the overall document. It can still be styled via CSS to sit over to the side if you choose to create a twin column layout.

The document <footer> section

This is the HTML5 document footer section where we load copyright and attribution data, along with a site RSS feed if you choose.

The {{ghost_foot}} tag and extra scripts

The {{ghost_foot}} tag is also critical and should be included at the end of the body section. Among other things, this tag loads the jQuery library.

If you are including JavaScript that depends on jQuery, as does our responsive_frames() function, it should hence be run after the {{ghost_foot}} tag.

Extra notes

We have a few CSS classes in place that can be used to style the theme, such as blog_title_lg applied to the blog title. Note the _lg appended to the class. This is an abbreviation for the *Learning Ghost* theme name, and is used to namespace classes to ensure that plugins that might bring in additional CSS don't conflict by inadvertently using identical class names.

You'll also see application of semantic HTML5 tags such as header, main, and footer, which we will be doing throughout, as well as WAI-ARIA roles for accessibility, and Schema.org markup for SEO. We won't go into great detail on these three things in this guide, but recommend you thoroughly read up on them to inform your development.

index.hbs

Insert the following code into the `index.hbs` file:

```
{{!< default}}

{{#foreach posts}}

<article role="article" itemscope itemtype="http://schema.org/
BlogPosting" class="{{post_class}}">

    <header>
       <time datetime="{{date format="YYYY-MM-DD"}}"
itemprop="datePublished">{{date format='dddd DD MMM YYYY'}}</time>
        <h1 class="post_title_list_lg" itemprop="headline"><a
href="{{{url}}}" rel="bookmark">{{{title}}}</a></h1>
    </header>

    {{excerpt}}

    <p><a href="{{url}}">Read More &rarr;</a></p>

    <footer>
      <p>{{{tags}}}</p>
    </footer>

</article>

{{/foreach}}

{{pagination}}
```

The preceding code is responsible for the display of your index area, that is, your paginated list of latest posts accessed via your homepage. This code is loaded into the default wrapper at the point the `{{{body}}}` tag was entered.

The {{!< default}} tag

This tag is essential for all template files other than `default.hbs` and should be placed on the very first line of each. The reason is that this tag tells Ghost that the template should be wrapped in the content of the `default.hbs` file.

The {{#foreach posts}}...{{/foreach}} block helper tags

These block helper tags iterate the `post` object, which holds all of the data pertaining to the page's current list of posts. Everything that appears between these opening and closing tags will be repeated for each post displayed.

The {{post_class}} tag

This tag will output different CSS classes per post, with the default output being a class of `post` and additional classes being added for each tag applied to the post in the format `tag-<tagname>`.

The {{date}} tag

There are two options for how the date of publishing can be output. Either a relative time can be shown, for example **1 month ago**, or the actual date can be shown, for example, **Thursday 15th May 2014**.

To show a relative time, place the date tag as follows:

```
{{date timeago="true"}}
```

To show the actual date, use the tag like this:

```
{{date format="dddd DD MMM YYYY"}}
```

When using the actual date the exact way, its output can be controlled with different settings in the `format` option, which determine how the date is formatted by a script Ghost uses named `Moment.js`. See the Moment.js date formatting guide for details on the options available.

The {{url}} tag

This tag outputs the URL of the post's individual post. It can be used to create *Read More* links, social sharing links, and so on.

By default, it will output a relative URL, for example, `/post-slug/`, but it can also output an absolute URL, for example, `http://www.yourdomain.com/post-slug/` by setting the absolute option to `true`:

```
{{url absolute="true"}}
```

This is useful to create social sharing links, as you'll see in the subsequent `post.hbs` section.

The {{title}} tag

This tag simply displays the title of the post.

The {{excerpt}} and {{content}} tags

In both the index area and the tag archive area, there are two ways of displaying the body of the post: the {{excerpt}} tag and the {{content}} tag.

The excerpt tag displays a clipped portion of the post, with length determined either in words or characters, and all HTML stripped. This prevents things such as images or videos being shown, so the excerpt is text only. By default, it shows the first 50 words. To show a different content, use either the words or characters option:

```
{{excerpt words="80"}}
{{excerpt characters="140"}}
```

The other option is the {{content}} tag which does not strip any HTML and shows the fully formatted post body with whatever images and videos that might be included. By default, the tag shows the whole post body but it too can be limited by either words or characters:

```
{{content words="80"}}
{{content characters="140"}}
```

The {{{tags}}} tag

This outputs all the tags applied to the current post, with each one automatically linked to the archive for that tag. Optionally, a prefix, separator, and suffix for the list of tags can be included, each of which can accept HTML, for example:

```
{{{tags prefix="<strong>Tagged with: </strong><em>" separator=" | "
suffix="</em>"}}}
```

 Note that if you do use HTML as per the preceding example, you will need to use triple curly braces to ensure it renders as expected.

The {{pagination}} tag

In the index and tag archive areas, the number of posts shown per page is set via Ghost's Posts per page admin field. Whenever there are more posts than the number saved under this setting, the {{pagination}} tag will output links reading **Older posts** and **Newer Posts** as well as a display showing **Page <current> of <total>**.

post.hbs

Insert the following code into the post.hbs file:

```
{{!< default}}

{{#post}}

<article role="article" itemscope itemtype="http://schema.org/
BlogPosting" class="{{post_class}}">

    <header>
      <time datetime="{{date format="YYYY-MM-DD"}}"
itemprop="datePublished">{{date format="dddd DD MMM YYYY"}}</time>
      <h1 itemprop="headline">{{{title}}}</h1>
    </header>

    {{content}}

    <footer>
      <p>{{{tags}}}</p>

      <address itemscope itemtype="https://schema.org/Person">
        {{#if author.image}}<div class="authorimage_nix"><img
src="{{author.image}}" itemprop="image" /></div>{{/if}}
        <h4 class="nix_author">{{#unless author.image}}<i class="nix_
icon-user"></i>{{/unless}}<span itemprop="author">{{{author.name}}}</
span></h4>
        {{#if author.website}}<p><a href="{{author.website}}"
itemprop="url" target="_blank" rel="author">{{author.website}}</a></
p>{{/if}}
        {{#if author.location}}<div itemscope itemtype="https://
schema.org/PostalAddress"><span itemprop="addressLocality">{{{author.
location}}}</span></div>{{/if}}
      </address>

      {{#if author.bio}}
        {{{author.bio}}}
      {{/if}}

      <section class="share">
        <h4>Share this post</h4>
        <a class="icon-twitter" href="http://twitter.com/
share?text={{encode title}}&url={{url absolute="true"}}"
          onclick="window.open(this.href, 'twitter-share',
'width=550,height=235');return false;">
          Twitter
        </a>
        <a class="icon-facebook" href="https://www.facebook.com/
sharer/sharer.php?u={{url absolute="true"}}"
```

```
            onclick="window.open(this.href, 'facebook-share','width=580,
height=296');return false;">
            Facebook
         </a>
         <a class="icon-google-plus" href="https://plus.google.com/
share?url={{url absolute="true"}}"
            onclick="window.open(this.href, 'google-plus-share',
'width=490,height=530');return false;">
            Google+
         </a>
      </section>
   </footer>

</article>

{{/post}}
```

This code controls the display of single posts viewed at their own URLs. You'll see many of the same template tags here as you saw in the previous two templates.

The primary differences in how you'll create your post.hbs file versus your index.hbs file are:

- No block helper loop is required as there's only one post. Instead, use the {{post}}...{{/post}} tags to output the single post.
- No need to link the title as you're already at the posts URL.
- Inclusion of author profile information and social sharing links.

The {{author}} object

The following properties of the {{author}} object can all be accessed via Handlebars paths, as was done in the default section with the {{blog}} object:

- {{{author.name}}}: This will output the author name string
- {{{author.location}}}: This will output the author location string
- {{{author.bio}}}: This will output the author bio string
- {{author.website}}: This will output the URL from author "website" field
- {{author.image}}: This will output the author image URL
- {{author.cover}}: This will give an output of the author cover image URL

 The first three properties will use triple curly braces to allow users to include HTML.

tag.hbs

Insert the following code into the `tag.hbs` file:

```
{{!< default}}

<div class="tag_archive_name_lg">
<h1>{{tag.name}}</h1>
</div>

{{#foreach posts}}

<article role="article" itemscope itemtype="http://schema.org/
BlogPosting" class="{{post_class}}">

    <header>
       <time datetime="{{date format="YYYY-MM-DD"}}"
itemprop="datePublished">{{date format='dddd DD MMM YYYY'}}</time>
       <h2 class="post_title_list_lg" itemprop="headline"><a
href="{{{url}}}" rel="bookmark">{{{title}}}</a></h2>
    </header>

    {{excerpt}}

    <p><a href="{{url}}">Read More &rarr;</a></p>

    <footer>
       {{{tags}}}
    </footer>

</article>

{{/foreach}}

{{pagination}}
```

In our base theme shell, the only difference between the tag archive and the index is the inclusion of {{tag.name}} in order to output the name of the tag whose archive is being viewed.

The `tag.hbs` template is most handy if you decide to have its presentation formatted differently for specific tags, such as `video` and `image`.

page.hbs

Insert the following code into the page.hbs file:

```
{{!< default}}

{{#post}}

<article role="article" class="{{post_class}}">

    <header>
      <h1 itemprop="headline">{{{title}}}</h1>
    </header>

    {{content}}

</article>

{{/post}}
```

The page template is functionally very similar to the post template, but stripped down and simplified. Static pages are designed to display basic information such as *About Us* or *Contact Details* and as such the only thing shown is the page title and its content.

Author information is accessible via this template, so it can be included if you wish.

Adding test content and activating your theme

You now have all the essential files and code in place in your theme, so it's ready to be activated. Before you do, however, we'll add some test content to your Ghost installation so you have something to build your theme around.

In the source files accompanying this guide, you'll find a ZIP file containing test content. Unzip it so you can get at the .json file inside. In your local Ghost installation, go to http://localhost:2368/ghost/debug/ then browse for the test content .json file and click on the **Import** button. This will add a selection of posts, tags, and some default author info to your installation.

Now, head to `Settings | General` and look at the drop-down list labeled `Theme`. In that list, you should now see `Learning Ghost - 0.1.0.` Select it and then save your settings. Now go to the homepage of your installation and refresh. Your homepage should now look like this:

Ghost

Just a blogging platform.

Thursday 10 Oct 2013

Post with Text

Lorem ipsum dolor sit amet, consectetuer adipiscing elit. Sed eleifend urna eu sapien. Quisque posuere nunc eu massa. Praesent bibendum lorem non leo. Morbi volutpat, urna eu fermentum rutrum, ligula lacus interdum mauris, ac pulvinar libero pede a enim. Etiam commodo malesuada ante. Donec nec ligula. Curabitur mollis semper diam

Read More →

Saturday 21 Sep 2013

Ordered List

Nulla sagittis convallis arcu. Sed sed nunc. Curabitur consequat. Quisque metus enim, venenatis fermentum, mollis in, porta et, nibh. Duis vulputate elit in elit. Mauris dictum libero id justo. Fusce in est. Sed nec diam. Pellentesque habitant morbi tristique senectus et netus et malesuada fames ac turpis egestas. Quisque semper

Read More →

Uncategorized

Thursday 12 Sep 2013

Quotes and Double Quotes

Lorem ipsum dolor sit amet, consectetuer adipiscing elit. Curabitur quam augue, vehicula quis, tincidunt vel, varius vitae, nulla. Sed convallis orci. Duis libero orci, pretium a, convallis quis, pellentesque a, dolor. Curabitur vitae nisi non dolor vestibulum consequat. Proin vestibulum. Ut ligula. Nullam sed dolor id odio volutpat pulvinar. Integer

Read More →

The shell of your theme is now entirely in place and you're ready to start applying the choices you made when completing your quick start theme quiz earlier.

Summary

So we have taken a look into the building blocks that make up a Ghost theme, looking at how to plan what theme you want on your Ghost blog, and what elements can be themed. From this, we've designed a theme shell; the blank canvas into which you'll apply all your design skills to create a great Ghost theme.

In the next chapter, we'll be exploring how to do this!

5
Applying Design Choices and Visual Styling

With your theme shell created, and your answers to the quick start theme quiz mapped out, you're now ready to apply the choices you made to your theme. We'll be doing this through a combination of working with the Stylus files in your project source folder, and making additions and edits to your theme's template files.

We'll begin with a rundown of how the Stylus files in your project folder operate, so you know what type of code to add where. We'll then cover implementation of each of the choices laid out in the quick start theme quiz. Finally, you'll be given an example of how to lay a unique visual style over the theme you've created and how to make it fully responsive to any resolution.

This chapter includes:

- Overview of the Stylus project file structure
- Applying the quick start theme quiz choices:
  - Default:
    - Single or twin column overall layout
    - Using the blog cover image as a site, header or sidebar background
    - Header height control in single column layouts
  - Index & Tag Archive:
    - Showing full or trimmed content and featured images / videos
    - Zebra striping
    - Featured post ordering and styling
    - Specifically tagged post styling

- ° Tag Archive:
  - ° Styling whole tag archive pages differently for specific tags
- ° Post & Page:
  - ° Post header style in single column layouts
- ° Post:
  - ° Styling featured single posts
  - ° Styling specifically tagged single posts
- • Adding unique visual styling:
  - ° Adding icon fonts
  - ° Setting image fallbacks
  - ° Example design: twin column visual styling
  - ° Example responsiveness: twin column design media queries
  - ° Overview of Stylus project file structure

Stylus files

You're about to start applying CSS to your theme, so before we move on, let's take a quick look at how the Stylus files (you'll find in your `LearningGhostSource` folder) work.

The import_stylus.styl file

This file imports the other Stylus files of the project, in the order specified therein. The order of import determines that the order code will be written into the actual production style sheet.

The meta folder

This folder contains the modified version of `Normalize.css` as well as any global variables, functions, and so on that need to be accessible throughout the project.

The vars_mixins_etc folder

In this folder, you will find three files, each containing any variables, mixins, functions, hashes, and any other code that is not an actual CSS style. The files are:

- `typography.styl`
- `layout.styl`
- `color_and_bgs.styl`

These files allow you to keep your project clearly organized along purpose-oriented lines. The driving principle is that once your design is complete, you should be able to easily adjust its typography, layout and colors/backgrounds purely by changing the values of variables defined in these three files.

Note the color variables you'll find at the beginning of the `colors_and_bgs.styl` file. There are five colors already defined which comprise a basic color scheme and you can adjust these variables to easily update your entire site as you go along.

To make it easy to know which file a particular mixin comes from, all typography mixins end in `_type()`, all layout mixins end in `_layout()`, and all colors and bgs mixins end in `_color()`.

As you add Stylus code to your files, make sure you have the correct use of indentation, that is, using tabs not spaces. If you are copying and pasting code into your Stylus files, please do so from the provided code samples to ensure that the tab indentations are added correctly.

The styles folder

The files in these folders draw in the information defined in the `vars_mixins_etc` folder and place it along with other raw CSS into the actual styles that will be written into your style sheet. The three files inside are:

- `element_defaults.styl`: This file outputs style defaults for HTML elements such as `body`, `img`, `H1`, and `H2`
- `custom_classes.styl`: This file outputs any custom CSS classes defined uniquely to the theme, for example, `.blog_title_lg`
- `media_queries.styl`: This file handles media queries used for responsive adjustment to various viewport sizes.

You'll see more about how all these files work in practice as we move into the next section.

Applying the quick start theme quiz choices

In this section, you'll be able to build up your theme design piece by piece, starting with aspects that affect the `default.hbs` template and moving on to each individual template. As you go, you can choose the sections that correspond to your quick start theme quiz choices, and hence have the ability to create several different types of designs via different combinations of the below.

Before you begin, run the `grunt watch` command on your project's compiler as per the instructions in *Chapter 3, Preparing for Theme Development*.

Note that, by default, your `screen.css` file will be written in compressed format to make its load speed as fast as possible; however, if you want it to be readable during development, change the compiler folder's Gruntfile `compress` option to `false` before running the `grunt watch` command.

As you hash out the initial layout stages, don't worry if your theme looks plain, because we'll be using only placeholder colors and visual styling to begin with. The idea is to get your layout and essential functionality in place first, then add a unique design style to fit over the top.

There are a lot of tips and tricks you can use in this section, so you don't necessarily need to read and absorb everything in one go. You can follow only the sections you need for the specific theme you're designing, and you can come back and refer to a different set of sections for your next theme when you come to it.

The default themes

Let's look at the overall default themes first.

Overall layout – single column

Your theme is already in a single column in the sense that the header sits on top of the posts which sits on top of the footer. However, it's currently too wide and hence too difficult for a visitor to read. It also has some gaps between the header, posts area, and footer that aren't supposed to be there, as well as no padding on the interior of any of the elements. To fix all these issues add these mixins to the bottom of `layout.styl`:

```
readable_column_layout()
    width 100%
```

```
    max-width readable_column_width
    clearfix()
    align_this(center)

blog_header_layout()
  padding-left unit( add_hpadding, rem)
  padding-right unit( add_hpadding, rem)
  padding-top unit( golden, rem)
  padding-bottom unit( add_vpadding, rem)

posts_area_layout()
  padding-top unit( golden, rem)
  padding-bottom unit( golden, rem)

post_layout()
  padding-left unit( add_hpadding, rem)
  padding-right unit( add_hpadding, rem)
  padding-top unit( golden, rem)
  padding-bottom unit( golden, rem)

tag_archive_name_layout()
  padding-left unit( add_hpadding, rem)
  padding-right unit( add_hpadding, rem)
  padding-top unit( golden, rem)
  padding-bottom unit( golden, rem)

pagination_layout()
  padding-left unit( add_hpadding, rem)
  padding-right unit( add_hpadding, rem)
  padding-top unit( golden, rem)
  padding-bottom unit( golden, rem)

blog_footer_layout()
  padding-left unit( add_hpadding, rem)
  padding-right unit( add_hpadding, rem)
  padding-top unit( golden, rem)
  padding-bottom unit( golden, rem)
```

The `readable_column_layout()` mixin works by taking the `readable_width` variable (already set to `40em` in your `layout.styl` file by default) and adding horizontal padding to it via the `add_hpadding` variable (set to five times the golden ratio by default). This is done via a calculation also already present in your `layout.style` file:

```
readable_column_width = readable_width + 2 * add_hpadding
```

The value of the the golden ratio is saved at `meta/global.styl` under the `golden` variable. Read about the golden ratio's long history of aesthetic application at `http://en.wikipedia.org/wiki/Golden_ratio#Applications_and_observations`.

If you want to change the overall width of your layout, just change the `readable_width` variable, and likewise if you want to change the horizontal padding amount, change the `add_hpadding` value.

The use of the `clearfix()` mixin, a built-in part of the Stylus Nib mixin library (`http://visionmedia.github.io/nib/`), ensures that the spaces between the header, posts area, and footer are removed.

The `blog_header_layout()`, `posts_area_layout()`, `post_layout()`, `tag_archive_name_layout()`, `pagination_layout()`, and `blog_footer_layout()` mixins add padding to the header, posts area, articles, pagination, and footer based on the `golden`, `add_hpadding` and `add_vpadding` variables.

We also want to add some basic color differentiation between the header, posts area, and footer to help you see where each section starts and finishes. There are already some prewritten color mixins in the `color_and_bgs.styl` file, so we'll apply those to the design now.

Apply the layout and color mixins to the theme by adding this code to the bottom of `custom_classes.styl`:

```
.blog_header_lg
    blog_header_color()
    blog_header_layout()

.posts_area_lg
    posts_area_color()
    posts_area_layout()

.post
    post_layout()

.tag_archive_name
  tag_archive_name_layout()

.pagination
    pagination_layout()

.blog_footer_lg
```

```
    blog_footer_color()
    blog_footer_layout()

.blog_header_lg
.posts_area_lg
.blog_footer_lg
    readable_column_layout()
```

Your theme will now look like this:

You'll also notice that this function is used in the `readable_column_layout()` mixin:

```
align_this(center)
```

This automatically aligns your columns centrally. If you would like to left or right align them instead, simply change the value in between the parenthesis to `align_this(left)` or `align_this(right)`.

Overall layout – twin column

In order to have the header section align to the one side, and the posts area and footer align to the other, we'll need to make a small addition to the `default.hbs` template. This will be to create a wrapper that prevents the elements aligning flush with the left and right sides of the screen.

Above the comment that reads {{! Document header }}, add this opening `div`:

```
<div class="wrap_lg">
```

After the closing `</footer>` tag, add a closing `div`:

```
</div>
```

Now, add the following new variables to your `layout.styl` file, under the `readable_column_width` variable:

```
sidebar_width = 33%
add_sidebar_hpadding = 3 * golden
readable_column_percentage = 100% - sidebar_width
total_width = (readable_column_width / readable_column_percentage) *
100
```

The first variable here lets you set the width you'd like your sidebar to be as a percentage of your layout's overall width. You can set it to anything you want, as long as it's a percentage value. By using a percentage value, the sidebar can flexibly adjust depending on viewport width.

The second line allows us to add some horizontal padding to the sidebar.

The third line calculates the width your readable columns should be as a percentage, by simply subtracting the width of the sidebar from 100 percent.

The last line then figures out what the total width of your layout should be in order to keep the readable column to the width set under the `readable_column_width` variable.

These extra lines mean you can still change the value of the `readable_column_width` variable to any `em` value you want, and the `sidebar_width` variable to any percentage you want, and the rest of your layout will be calculated automatically.

If you already have a `readable_column_layout()` mixin in your `layout.styl` file, delete it, then add the following mixins:

```
readable_column_layout()
    width readable_column_percentage
```

```
        float left

    sidebar_layout()
        absolute top right
        bottom 0
        width sidebar_width
        padding-left unit( add_sidebar_hpadding, rem)
        padding-right unit( add_sidebar_hpadding, rem)

    wrapper_layout()
        width 100%
        min-height 100%
        max-width total_width
        position relative
        align_this(center)
        clearfix()
```

Also, ensure that the `blog_header_layout()`, `posts_area_layout()`, `post_layout()`, `pagination_layout()`, and `blog_footer_layout()` mixins from the previous sections are included, if you haven't already added them.

Note that the above will put the sidebar in the right, and the posts area and footer on the left. If you would like them the other way around, change `readable_column()` to `float right` and `sidebar()` to `absolute top left`. (This uses the `absolute` seamless mixin from the Nib library.)

The next step is to apply these mixins via your `custom_classes.styl` file.

If you already have code in place from trying out the single column layout, delete everything but the `.post_title_list_lg` class and then add this new code:

```
    .wrap_lg
        wrapper_layout()

    .blog_header_lg
        blog_header_color()
        blog_header_layout()
        sidebar_layout()

    .posts_area_lg
        posts_area_color()
        posts_area_layout()
        readable_column_layout()

    .post
        post_layout()

    .tag_archive_name_lg
```

```
    tag_archive_name_layout()

.pagination
    pagination_layout()

.blog_footer_lg
    blog_footer_color()
    blog_footer_layout()
    readable_column_layout()
```

The application of the `wrapper_layout()` mixin to the wrapper `div` we added to the `default.hbs` file will set the appropriate width to the overall area, and will also clear the floats of the elements it contains.

Additionally, the wrapper `div` is centered via the `wrapper_layout()` mixin's use of `align_this(center)`. As with a single column layout, if you would prefer to left or right align your design, simply change the value passed through `align_this()`.

On executing a refresh operation, your layout will now look like this:

Use the blog cover image – as site background

You can have your theme use the blog cover image equally well as a site background with a single column or twin column background.

First, open up your `default.hbs` template file and find the opening body tag, which by default uses this code:

```
<body class="{{body_class}}">
```

Then replace the preceding line with this:

```
<body class="{{body_class}}" {{#if @blog.cover}}style="background-
image: url({{@blog.cover}});"{{/if}}>
```

This checks to see if a blog cover image is available, and if available, sets it as the background image for the body.

Next, open up the `color_and_bgs.styl` file from the `vars_mixins_etc` folder of your project source. Update your `body_color()` mixin by adding the following code:

```
body_color()
    background-color color_01
    color color_02
    background-repeat no-repeat
    background-position center center
    background-attachment fixed
    background-size cover
```

This code tells the background image to fit to the viewport size, and to remain still when the user scrolls up and down.

Find a large image you can use as a test background and set it via the Ghost admin as your site's blog cover. In our examples, we're using *September in the Forest* by Larisa Koshkina from PublicDomainPictures.net (`http://www.publicdomainpictures.net/view-image.php?image=25507`).

Refresh and, on a single column layout, you should see something like this:

Use the blog cover image as the header background for a single column and a sidebar background for a twin column.

Essentially, the same technique as above is used to set the blog cover as the header/sidebar background.

In the `default.hbs` template, find the opening `<header>` tag, which by default is:

```
<header class="blog_header_lg" role='banner' itemscope
itemtype='http://schema.org/WPHeader'>
```

Then replace the preceding line of code with this:

```
<header class="blog_header_lg" {{#if @blog.cover}}style="background-
image: url({{@blog.cover}});"{{/if}} role='banner' itemscope
itemtype='http://schema.org/WPHeader'>
```

 If you have already applied the blog cover image to the site background, set your opening body tag back to the default first.

Again, this checks for the presence of a blog cover image and sets it as the background if available.

Then, update the `blog_header_color()` mixin in the `color_and_bgs.styl` file to the following:

```
blog_header_color()
  background-color darken(color_05, 2.5%)
  background-repeat no-repeat
  background-position right top
  background-attachment fixed
  background-size cover
  a:link,
  a:visited
    color color_01
```

This sets the image to fill the `<header>` section's background, and also lightens the color of the text therein, so it can be read on the darkened background.

If you are using a twin column layout, it will now look something like this:

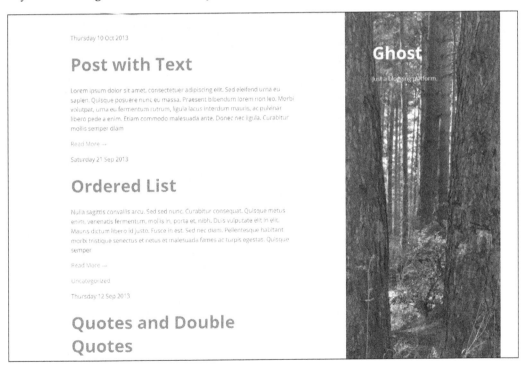

The background image will remain in a fixed position due to the `background-attachment fixed` line in the `blog_header_color()` mixin. This prevents any vertical repeating images or empty space.

Single column layout – header height auto

With the header code as you have so far, the header height will already automatically size itself to its content. With the blog cover in the background will look like this:

You may also wish to allow your header background to expand to the full width of the screen. To do this, we'll need to make another modification to the default.hbs file to add a full-width wrapper around the header that the background can be applied to.

Before the opening `<header>` tag, add the following line of code:

```
<div class="header_bg_lg">
```

If you would like the cover image applied to the background, make it:

```
<div class="header_bg_lg" {{#if @blog.cover}}style="background-image:
url({{@blog.cover}});"{{/if}}>
```

Close the `div` after closing the `</header>` tag:

```
</div>
```

If you have already followed the section above and added the blog cover to the background of your header section, set the opening `<header>` tag back to its default code:

```
<header class="blog_header_lg" role='banner' itemscope
itemtype='http://schema.org/WPHeader'>
```

Now, in your `custom_classes.styl` file, note the following code:

```
.blog_header_lg
    blog_header_color()
    blog_header_layout()
```

Replace it with the following code:

```
.header_bg_lg
    blog_header_color()


.blog_header_lg
    blog_header_layout()
```

This takes the `color` and `bg` settings that were applied to the header itself and applies them instead to the new wrapper `div`.

 If you want the header background to move when the user scrolls rather than remaining fixed, omit or comment out the `background-attachment fixed` line in the `blog_header_color()` mixin.

You'll now have this layout:

Single column layout – header height large

To set your header height to a large size, similar to the style of Casper, the default Ghost theme, add the following mixin to your `layout.styl` file:

```
blog_header_bg_layout()
    display table
    position relative
    width 100%
    height 60%
```

Then, in your `custom_classes.styl` file, apply the mixin to your `.header_bg_lg` class by updating it to the following:

```
.header_bg_lg
    blog_header_color()
    blog_header_bg_layout()
```

If you previously added the `<div class="wrap_lg">...</div>` tags used for the twin column layout to your `default.hbs` file, you will need to remove them for this technique to work.

To vertically and horizontally align the blog logo, title, and description within this large header space, update your `blog_header_layout()` mixin to the following:

```
blog_header_layout()
    padding-top unit( golden, rem)
    padding-bottom unit( add_vpadding, rem)
    display table-cell
    vertical-align middle
    text-align center
```

Your layout will now look like this:

Single column layout – full screen header

To have the header take up the full height of the screen in order to create the whole page blog cover, follow the same steps as in the previous section, with one significant difference. Instead of setting the head `blog_header_bg_layout()` mixin to `height 60%`, set it to `height 100%`:

```
blog_header_bg_layout()
    display table
    position relative
    width 100%
    height 100%
```

In order to make the title and description stand out a little more, add the following mixin to your `typography.styl` file:

```
blog_header_type()
    font-size 200%
    font-weight 700
    text-shadow 0.125em 0.125em 0.125em rgba(0, 0, 0, 0.7)
```

Then apply the mixin to your `.blog_header_lg` class in your `custom_classes.styl` file as follows:

```
.blog_header_lg
    blog_header_layout()
    blog_header_type()
```

With these new settings in place, you'll get an effect like this:

Index and tag archive

In this section, we are going to take a look at the different types of index and tag archives, their properties, and usage.

Posts – excerpt, full or trimmed

We've already covered how to use the {{excerpt}} and {{content}} tags in the *Creating your theme shell* section earlier on, so you can refer to that for a refresher.

The theme shell you have already created uses an {{excerpt}} tag with the default length of fifty words. If you use this or any other form of a shortened post, be sure to include some type of link through to the single post. In the theme as you have it so far, it is included in this form:

```
<p><a href="{{url}}">Read More &rarr;</a></p>
```

If you are using the {{content}} tag at its default of showing the entire post, a *Read More* functionality would not be required; however, you may wish to retain the link and change its display to Permalink instead, so people can grab the single post URL should they want to share it with friends.

If excerpt – show post's first image/video/soundcloud

If you're using an excerpt, HTML is trimmed to show text only. This means any images, videos, soundcloud embeds, and so on from within your post won't show on your index or tag archive pages. Therefore, you can choose to pull the first of these from your post and display it above your excerpt without worrying about an image or video appearing twice in one space.

To do this, place the following tag somewhere in between the <article>...</article> tags of your index.hbs and tag.hbs files, typically, directly above or below the <header>...</header> section:

```
{{content words="0"}}
```

Adding zebra striping – alternate colors every second post

To add zebra striping to your posts, find the opening. Now, replace the opening `<article>` tag of your `index.hbs` and `tag.hbs` files with:

```
<article role="article" itemscope itemtype="http://schema.org/
BlogPosting" class="{{post_class}} {{#if @even}}post_even_lg{{else}}
post_odd_lg{{/if}}">
```

This will add a class of `post_even_lg` to every second post, and `post_odd_lg` to every other post.

To set background colors for these, add the following mixins to your `color_and_bgs.styl` file:

```
post_even_color()
    background-color darken(color_05, 2.5%)

post_odd_color()
    background-color color_05
```

Then, add the following styles to your `custom_classes.styl` file:

```
.post_even_lg
    post_even_color()

.post_odd_lg
    post_odd_color()
```

You'll also most likely want to adjust the vertical padding of the posts area and the posts to better suit the zebra striping, using the `posts_area_layout()` and `post_layout()` mixins by changing them to:

```
posts_area_layout()
    padding 0

post_layout()
    padding-left unit( add_hpadding, rem)
    padding-right unit( add_hpadding, rem)
    padding-top unit( add_vpadding, rem)
    padding-bottom unit( add_vpadding, rem)
```

On performing refresh, you'll now see alternating background colors at the width of your posts:

If instead, you want the zebra striped backgrounds to stretch to the full width of the screen, you'll need to add a wrapper around the posts to which the background can apply.

Set your `index.hbs` and `tag.hbs` files' opening `<article>` tag back to its default code:

```
<article role="article" itemscope itemtype="http://schema.org/
BlogPosting" class="{{post_class}}">
```

Above the opening `<article>` tag, place the following:

```
<div class="{{#if @even}}post_even_lg{{else}}post_odd_lg{{/if}}">
```

Close the new post wrapper div after the closing `</article>` tag:

```
</div>
```

This code will now apply the zebra striping background colors to the wrapper instead of the post itself. Now, in order to allow those backgrounds to stretch full width, we have to allow the post area that wraps them to stretch to full width as well. However, we still want the actual posts to stay at readable width.

To achieve this, find this block of code in your `custom_classes.styl` file:

```
.blog_header_lg
.posts_area_lg
.blog_footer_lg
    readable_column_layout()
```

Change it to:

```
.blog_header_lg
.post
.pagination
.blog_footer_lg
    readable_column_layout()
```

Note that the `.posts_area_lg` class has been removed so the `readable_column()` mixin is no longer applied to it and hence no longer limits its width.

In its place, the `.post` and `.pagination` classes have been added so the mixin will now limit their widths and center them on the page.

If you'd like to also have the blog footer background full width, apply the same process that you already have to the header and posts; add a wrapper div around the footer element, apply the `blog_footer_color()` background styling mixin to that wrapper, and add the footer element's `.blog_footer_lg` class to the list of elements the mixin is applied to.

Featured posts – list first above default posts

By default, the `{{#foreach posts}}`...`{{/foreach}}` loop will show all your posts, whether featured or not, in chronological order. To list the featured posts first, you need to create two loops; one with the featured posts and the other with unfeatured posts:

1. To do this, in your `index.hbs` and `tag.hbs` files, make a duplicate of your entire `{{#foreach posts}}`...`{{/foreach}}` block.

2. After the opening `{{#foreach posts}}` of the first block, add this:

   `{{#if featured}}`

3. Then just before the closing `{{/foreach}}` of the first block add:

   `{{/if}}`

   This first loop will now output only featured posts.

4. Now, after the opening `{{#foreach posts}}` of the second block, add this:

   `{{#unless featured}}`

5. Then, just before the closing `{{/foreach}}` of the second block add:

   `{{/if}}`

   The second block will now output only posts that are not featured.

6. Set some of your test posts to the `Featured` status, refresh your site, and you'll see they now appear at the top of the post list.

Applying styles to featured posts

If you want to have featured posts styled differently to other posts, the easiest way is to work with the `.featured` class Ghost automatically adds to these posts.

In your `color_and_bgs.styl` file, create a mixin to control the styling of featured posts:

```
featured_post_color()
     background-color lighten(color_03, 10%)
```

Then apply that mixin to the `.featured` class by adding this to your `custom_classes.styl` file:

```
.featured
     featured_post_color()
```

With featured posts listed first and styled differently, you'll now have an effect like this:

Applying styles to the posts with certain tags

In the same way you can style featured posts differently, you can also style posts differently if a specific predetermined tag is applied to them.

For every tag that is applied to a post, a class of `tag-<tagname>` is added by Ghost. So you can easily create tag specific styles in your CSS using the same method as described previously for featured posts, that is, create mixin(s) to style the post differently, and then apply those mixins to a new class added to your `custom_classes.styl` file.

However, you can also have your theme output completely different code if a certain tag is detected using the {{#has}} block helper. Let's take a look at a basic example where we modify the presentation of video tagged posts.

In your index.hbs and tag.hbs files, add these lines after your opening {{#foreach posts}} tag:

```
{{#has tag="video"}}
```

```
{{else}}
```

Before your closing {{/foreach}} tag place:

```
{{/has}}
```

Now, in between the {{#has tag="video"}} and {{else}} tags place this:

```
<article role="article" itemscope itemtype="http://schema.org/
BlogPosting" class="{{post_class}}">

    {{content words="0"}}

    <div class="video_inner">

    <header>
       <h1 class="post_title_list_lg" itemprop="headline"><a
href="{{{url}}}" rel="bookmark">{{{title}}}</a></h1>
       <time datetime="{{date format="YYYY-MM-DD"}}"
itemprop="datePublished">{{date format="dddd DD MMM YYYY"}}</time>
    </header>

    <p><a href="{{url}}">Read About This Video &rarr;</a></p>

    <footer>
      <p>{{{tags}}}</p>
    </footer>

    </div>

</article>
```

The preceding code will now be used for any post bearing a `video` tag, while the code you already had in place will be used for any post that does not have this tag.

In your `layout.styl` file add this:

```
video_post_layout()
    padding 0
```

And in your `custom_classes.styl` file add:

```
.tag-video
    video_post_layout()

.video_inner
    post_layout()
```

What this does is remove all the padding from any video post, allowing the video to sit flush against the outer edges.

You'll notice that in the new code added to the index and tag template files, there is a `div` with the `video_inner` class wrapped around all the text content of that post. The `post_layout()` mixin is applied to that wrapper's class instead of the entire post. This means that while the video sits flush against the edges, the text content will still have spacing placed around it

Any posts tagged as `video` will now appear like this:

Tag archive

Style the whole tag archive page differently for specific tags.

In the same way you saw a single post tagged as `video` styled differently in the previous section, you can style an entire tag archive page differently for specific tags. So, for example, you could create a gallery of images when on the archive for the tag name `image`. I won't go into how to create a gallery specifically here, but I will give you the code required to set up your tag archive pages for unique styling.

There are two parts to this technique: styling the individual posts (so you can do things such as creating a grid layout with them) and styling the overall document (so you can do things such as allowing a grid to tile across the full width of the screen).

The individual posts can be styled with the exact same method as in the previous section, that is, in your `tags.hbs` file use the `{{#has tag="<tagname>"}}`...`{{/has}}` block helper to output different layout code depending on the current archive tag name. If you're on the `image` tag archive, you know all the posts will have the `image` tag, so they'll output in the same way.

 If you use this approach, be sure to tell the users of your theme to not apply more than one of the tags that you've created uniquely styled tag archives for. For example, if you've created an image gallery and a video gallery, make sure people know not to use both tags on one post.

In order to apply styling to the whole document, you'll need to add a custom class to the opening `<body>` tag, for example, `image_gallery`. You can then use that body class to control the styling of the entire page. To do this, we use what are known as **content blocks**.

For example, to set a body class of `image_gallery`, on the `image` tag archive, you would update your opening body tag to:

```
<body class="{{body_class}} {{block "customBodyClass"}}">
```

The `{{block "customBodyClass"}}` tag creates a placeholder that can be dynamically updated within your template files.

Then, in between the `{{#has tag="image"}}`...`{{/has}` tags, you will have added to your `tag.hbs` template file and set the value of `customBodyClass` to `image_gallery` as follows:

```
{{#has tag="image"}}

{{#contentFor "customBodyClass"}}image_gallery{{/contentFor}}
```

The image output code is as follows:

```
{{else}}
```

The non-image output code is as follows:

```
{{/has}}
```

Now, when a visitor is on the `image` tag archive page, the opening body tag will output as follows, giving you the ability to style the whole page uniquely:

```
<body class="archive-template image_gallery">
```

Post and page

In the previous sections, we've covered all of the little Ghost tag-driven tricks you can use to control the formatting of your theme. Let's now deep-dive into how to set up the header size of the page and deal with posts.

If single column layout AND header height full/large – post header style

One of the design options we've covered so far is the ability to have a large or full screen header area in a single column design. This is nice to welcome the visitor to your homepage, but you don't want that much space to be taken up with the header on your posts and static pages.

You should instead set the header to shrink down to an automated height in these areas, that is, fit to the logo, title, and description it contains. To enable you to do this, we'll again use a content block as we did in the last section, this time applied to the blog header.

If you are using a full width header background, add a content block class placeholder to your header wrapper div as shown in the following code:

```
<div class="header_bg_lg {{block "customHeaderClass"}}" {{#if @blog.
cover}}style="background-image: url({{@blog.cover}});"{{/if}}>
```

Alternatively, if you are not using a wrapper around your header, add the class directly to your opening header tag instead:

```
<header class="blog_header_lg {{block "customHeaderClass"}}"
role='banner' itemscope itemtype='http://schema.org/WPHeader'>
```

Then in your `post.hbs` and `page.hbs` files, anywhere after the `{{!< default}}` tag, add the following:

```
{{#contentFor "customHeaderClass"}}auto_height_lg{{/contentFor}}
```

This will add a class of `auto_height_lg` to your header when on a post or static page.

In your `layout.styl` file, add this new mixin:

```
auto_height_layout()
    height auto
```

And then apply it to the `auto_height_lg` class by adding the following to your `custom_classes.styl` file:

```
.auto_height_lg
    auto_height_layout()
```

Now, when a visitor is on a post or page, the header will only be the size it needs to be to accommodate its content.

Post

Now that we come to implementing the choices you made in the post section of your theme quiz, you've already learned the actual techniques to use in the previous sections. The only difference is you'll be applying the techniques within your `post.hbs` template file.

So instead of going into great detail on how to apply the techniques again to your `post.hbs` template, I'll give you a quick rundown of which techniques to use for each of your theme quiz choices.

- **Featured single post; style differently to default single post**

    Use the techniques described in the section on styling featured posts in your index and tag archive areas. If you have already applied featured post styling in those areas, the same styling will automatically apply in single post view too.

    If you want featured post styling on your single posts to be different to that of your index and tag archive, the easiest way is to use a `{{#if featured}}...{{/if}}` check in your `post.hbs` template file to output a custom class on the post.

- **Specifically tagged single post; style differently for certain tags**

  The techniques to style single posts differently, depending on tags, are essentially the same as used in the index and tag archive areas. As with featured posts, any styling applied to the index and tag archive areas will automatically be applied in the single post context too. However, if you need different HTML to be output for specific tags, remember to use the `{{#has tag="<tagname>"}}...{{/has}}` check in your `post.hbs` template to do so.

Adding unique visual styling

At this point, you should now have a fully functional theme with a completed layout, but with the same placeholder color scheme and visual styling you began with. Now, it's time to turn your bland looking theme into something visually unique.

90 percent of the visual styling from here is just a matter of working with the mixins you already have in place in your `typography.styl`, `layout.styl` and `color_and_bgs.styl` files. You can do a great deal just by adding custom values to the color variables and modifying the `_color()` mixins.

Of course, the actual designs you create will come down to your own unique talents and style so we can't teach you that here, but what we can do is give you an example of a design laid over the top of one of the layouts we've already covered earlier, along with the code used to create it so you can see what kind of things can be done.

Before moving onto that example, there are a couple of extra tricks you'll want to know about to help your visual styling process along.

Adding icon fonts

Casper, the default theme for Ghost, includes an awesome set of font files that give you icons for Ghost's own logo as well as RSS, Google+, Facebook, and Twitter. Instead of using static-sized icon images, you can use this font and your icons can then be sized and colored as you would any text-based content.

To add them to your theme, copy all the files from the `assets/fonts` folder of the Casper theme into the `assets/fonts` folder of your own theme.

The CSS code to enable this icon font is already in place in your project folder's `stylus/meta/global.styl` file, it just needs to be activated. Open the file and find this line of code:

```
use_icon_font = false
```

Change it to:

```
use_icon_font = true
```

You'll now automatically see icons in the social sharing section of your single posts and in your blog footer:

If you want to show only icons and not text, wrap the text labels of the above in span tags with the class, hidden_lg, for example:

```
<p><a class="subscribe icon-feed" href="{{@blog.url}}/rss/"><span
class="hidden_lg">Subscribe!</span></a></p>
```

Setting image fallbacks

If you're using the blog cover as an integral part of your theme design, or any other images set via Ghost's admin panel, that is, the logo, author image, author cover, then you may want to set fallback images that will appear if the user has not set their own.

To do this, check to see if there is a user set image, as we already did previously in the sections working with the blog cover:

```
{{#if @blog.cover}} style="background-image: url({{@blog.cover}});"
{{/if}}
```

Then, add a fallback image using the {{asset}} helper by adjusting that check as follows:

```
{{#if @blog.cover}} style="background-image: url({{@blog.cover}});"
{{else}} style="background-image: url( {{asset "images/default.jpg"}}
);" {{/if}}
```

Example design – twin column visual styling

Let's take a look at the layout which was created using the twin column layout settings described earlier, with the overall alignment set to the left, the header/sidebar also aligned to the left with its width set to 30 percent, and zebra striping in place.

 If you install this theme from the files accompanying this book, be sure to remove any blog cover image you may have already added via your Ghost admin area, so you can see the theme as pictured.

The layout has two small tweaks from the default twin column code, whereby the `sidebar_layout()` and `blog_header_layout()` mixins are altered in order to remove horizontal padding and center text.

The resulting `layout.styl` code is:

```
//**
// Vars
//**

hr_vmargin = golden
add_hpadding = 5 * golden
add_vpadding = 3 * golden
readable_width = 40em
```

```
readable_column_width = readable_width + 2 * add_hpadding

sidebar_width = 30%
add_sidebar_hpadding = 3 * golden
readable_column_percentage = 100% - sidebar_width
total_width = (readable_column_width / readable_column_percentage) *
100

//**
// Functions
//**

align_this(align)
  if align is center
    margin-left auto
    margin-right auto
  else if align is left
    margin-left 0
    margin-right auto
  else if align is right
    margin-left auto
    margin-right 0

// layout - mixins
readable_column_layout()
  width readable_column_percentage
  float right

sidebar_layout()
  absolute top left
  bottom 0
  width sidebar_width
  text-align center

wrapper_layout()
  width 100%
  min-height 100%
  max-width total_width
  position relative
  align_this(left)
  clearfix()

blog_header_layout()
  padding 0

posts_area_layout()
  padding 0

post_layout()
  padding-left unit( add_hpadding, rem)
```

```
    padding-right unit( add_hpadding, rem)
    padding-top unit( add_vpadding, rem)
    padding-bottom unit( add_vpadding, rem)

tag_archive_name_layout()
    padding-left unit( add_hpadding, rem)
    padding-right unit( add_hpadding, rem)
    padding-top unit( golden, rem)
    padding-bottom unit( golden, rem)

pagination_layout()
    padding-left unit( add_hpadding, rem)
    padding-right unit( add_hpadding, rem)
    padding-top unit( golden, rem)
    padding-bottom unit( golden, rem)

blog_footer_layout()
    padding-left unit( add_hpadding, rem)
    padding-right unit( add_hpadding, rem)
    padding-top unit( golden, rem)
    padding-bottom unit( golden, rem)
```

The blog cover image used is named *Fresh Spring Background* and comes from `www.publicdomainpictures.net`, which is an excellent source of images to practise your theming techniques with.

The visual styling was created entirely by setting this content in the `color_and_bgs.styl` file:

```
//**
// Color vars
//**

color_01 = #F7F4EA
color_02 = #424242
color_03 = #C2C983
color_04 = #E0BC72
color_05 = #000

//**
// Mixins
//**

body_color()
    background-color color_01
    color color_02
    background-repeat no-repeat
    background-position center center
    background-attachment fixed
```

```
        background-size cover

    link_color()
        color darken(color_03, 20%)

    link_hover_color()
        color color_04

    blog_header_color()
      background-color rgba(color_05, 0.875)
      border-right 0.25rem solid rgba(color_05, 0.9)
      a:link,
      a:visited
        color color_03

    posts_area_color()
        background-color rgba(color_01, 0.3)
        border-right 0.25rem solid color_03

    blog_footer_color()
        border-top 0.0625rem solid color_03
        background-color darken(color_01, 5%)
        border-right 0.25rem solid color_03

    post_even_color()
        background-color rgba(color_01, 0.7)
        border-bottom 0.0625rem solid rgba(color_03, 0.5)

    post_odd_color()
        border-bottom 0.0625rem solid rgba(color_03, 0.5)
```

There is also a small addition to the theme's typography, whereby the Google Font *Lobster Two* is applied to the blog title and it is made larger. First, the Google font is loaded into the theme in the default.hbs file:

```
<link href='//fonts.googleapis.com/css?family=Open+Sans:400,700,400ita
lic,700italic|Lobster+Two:700italic' rel='stylesheet' type='text/css'>
```

In the typography.styl file, this code is added:

```
blog_title_font = "Lobster Two"

blog_title_type()
    font-family blog_title_font
    font-size 6rem
```

The font is applied to the blog title by adding this to the custom_classes.styl file:

```
.blog_title_lg
    blog_title_type()
```

The `post_even_color()` mixin is also applied to the tag archive's title to differentiate it from the posts area. The entire `custom_classes.styl` file thus ends up as follows:

```
//**
// Styles
//**

// Standardize Index and Tag Archive post titles
.post_title_list_lg
  post_title_list_type()

.wrap_lg
  wrapper_layout()

.blog_header_lg
  blog_header_color()
  blog_header_layout()
  sidebar_layout()

.posts_area_lg
  posts_area_color()
  posts_area_layout()
  readable_column_layout()

.post
  post_layout()

.tag_archive_name_lg
  tag_archive_name_layout()
  post_even_color()

.pagination
  pagination_layout()

.blog_footer_lg
  blog_footer_color()
  blog_footer_layout()
  readable_column_layout()

.post_even_lg
  post_even_color()

.post_odd_lg
  post_odd_color()

.blog_title_lg
  blog_title_type()
```

So, as you can see, thanks to the groundwork already laid, it takes very little code to add an entire design style to your theme.

Example responsiveness – twin column design media queries

Your theme already has responsiveness in place for both images and anything placed in an iframe, such as videos and soundcloud embeds. The only thing remaining is to add media queries to ensure the layout works well at all screen sizes.

The technique to achieve this is quite straightforward. You simply open up the `media_queries.styl` file from the `stylus/styles` folder of your project source and add media queries at each point your design breaks as you shrink it. These points will be arbitrary depending on the specifics of the design.

 We personally use a script named RDBL to help me handle the assessment of where breakpoints should be. If you'd like to do the same, the script is free on Github at `https://github.com/polygonix/RDBL`.

This stage of your theme creation process should always occur after your default design is complete; otherwise, you won't be able to account for all elements of the layout.

For example, the following code is all that's required to make our example twin column design fully responsive:

```
@media (max-width: 71.187em)
  //reduce blog title font size
  .blog_title_lg
    font-size 5rem

  //reduce h padding
  .post
  .tag_archive_name_lg
  .pagination
  .blog_footer_lg
    padding-left unit( add_hpadding * 0.75, rem)
    padding-right unit( add_hpadding * 0.75, rem)

@media (max-width: 62.687em)
  //reduce blog title font size
  .blog_title_lg
    font-size 4rem

  //reduce h padding
  .post
  .tag_archive_name_lg
```

```
  .pagination
  .blog_footer_lg
    padding-left unit( add_hpadding * 0.5, rem)
    padding-right unit( add_hpadding * 0.5, rem)

@media (max-width: 56.812em)
  //reduce blog title font size
  .blog_title_lg
    font-size 3rem

  //reduce h padding
  .post
  .tag_archive_name_lg
  .pagination
  .blog_footer_lg
    padding-left unit( add_hpadding * 0.25, rem)
    padding-right unit( add_hpadding * 0.25, rem)
@media (max-width: 51.125em)
  //convert to single column
  //move header to the top, add vpadding and add left border to
balance right border
  .blog_header_lg
    position static
    width 100%
    padding-top unit( golden, rem)
    padding-bottom unit( add_vpadding, rem)
    border-left 0.25rem solid rgba(color_05, 0.9)

  //move posts area and footer below header and add border to left
side to match right
  .posts_area_lg
  .blog_footer_lg
    float none
    width 100%
    border-left 0.25rem solid color_03

  //increase blog title font-size again now there's more horizontal
space
  .blog_title_lg
    font-size 4rem
    padding-top unit( golden, rem)
    padding-bottom unit( golden, rem)

  //increase h padding agin now there's more room
  .post
    padding-left unit( add_hpadding * 0.75, rem)
    padding-right unit( add_hpadding * 0.75, rem)
```

```
          padding-top unit( golden, rem)
          padding-bottom unit( golden, rem)

        .tag_archive_name_lg
        .pagination
        .blog_footer_lg
          padding-left unit( add_hpadding * 0.75, rem)
          padding-right unit( add_hpadding * 0.75, rem)

    @media (max-width: 44em)
      //reduce h padding
      .post
      .tag_archive_name_lg
      .pagination
      .blog_footer_lg
        padding-left unit( add_hpadding * 0.5, rem)
        padding-right unit( add_hpadding * 0.5, rem)

    @media (max-width: 39.937em)
      //getting thin now so remove borders
      .blog_header_lg
      .posts_area_lg
      .blog_footer_lg
        border-left 0
        border-right 0

      //reduce h padding
      .post
      .tag_archive_name_lg
      .pagination
      .blog_footer_lg
        padding-left unit( add_hpadding * 0.25, rem)
        padding-right unit( add_hpadding * 0.25, rem)

    //set the min resolution width you want to cater for
    @media (max-width: 480px)
      html
        min-width 480px
```

The purpose of each of the adjustments made via these media queries is described in the comments throughout.

In a nutshell, the preceding code makes sure the design is viewport optimized and is easily readable at any resolution between the layout's maximum width and a minimum of 480 px.

At 1024 px resolution, the screen looks like this:

Just a blogging platform.

Thursday 10 Oct 2013

Post with Text

Lorem ipsum dolor sit amet, consectetuer adipiscing elit. Sed eleifend urna eu sapien. Quisque posuere nunc eu massa. Praesent bibendum lorem non leo. Morbi volutpat, urna eu fermentum rutrum, ligula lacus interdum mauris, ac pulvinar libero pede a enim. Etiam commodo malesuada ante. Donec nec ligula. Curabitur mollis semper diam.

Duis viverra nibh a felis condimentum pretium. Nullam tristique lacus non purus. Donec vel felis. Etiam et sapien. Pellentesque nec quam a justo tincidunt laoreet. Aenean id enim. Donec lorem arcu, eleifend venenatis, rhoncus mollis, semper at, dui. Praesent velit tellus, adipiscing et, blandit convallis, dictum at, dui. Integer suscipit tortor in orci. Phasellus consequat. Quisque dictum convallis pede.

Mauris viverra scelerisque mauris. Nulla facilisis, elit malesuada pretium egestas, dolor arcu commodo est, at egestas massa tortor ut ante. Etiam eget libero. Aenean pretium, tellus sed sodales semper, turpis purus aliquet orci, pulvinar ornare odio tortor sit amet dui.

Aenean id orci. Cum sociis natoque penatibus et magnis dis parturient montes, nascetur ridiculus mus. Vivamus magna. Mauris tincidunt iaculis enim. Duis a mi vitae sapien dapibus tincidunt. Proin metus.

Proin cursus, libero non auctor faucibus, urna mi vestibulum orci, sit amet fermentum nibh purus eget enim. Aenean aliquet ligula

At 768 px resolution, the screen looks like this:

At 480 px resolution, the screen looks like this:

Summary

This coverage of the full gamut of options offered via the Ghost theme API shows that while working with Ghost may be very simple and straightforward compared to other platforms, there is a wide array of possibilities already available. This is despite the fact that API is still in its early days and we can expect to see more features added as time goes on.

You're equipped with everything there is to know about the Ghost theme API and the various ways you can take advantage of it. Every trick in the book, and some that aren't, has been covered here so you'll have plenty of variety you can inject into your theme designs.

When you feel confident to share your themes, you can go ahead and submit them to the Ghost theme marketplace for others to use. You don't have to be a theme seller to share your themes here, as a price tag of *free* is perfectly acceptable. At the same time, of course, if you do wish to sell your themes, the Ghost marketplace is the perfect place to start.

Have a great time theming for Ghost!

Markdown Syntax and Ghost Shortcut Keys

The following table is taken from Ghost's post-editing inline help:

Result	Markdown	Shortcut
Bold	`**text**`	*Ctrl / Cmd + B*
Emphasize	`*text*`	*Ctrl / Cmd + I*
Inline code	`` `code` ``	*Cmd + K / Ctrl + Shift + K*
Strike-through	`~~text~~`	*Ctrl + Alt + U*
Link	`[title](http://)`	*Ctrl + Shift + L*
Image	`![alt](http://)`	*Ctrl + Shift + I*
List	`* item`	*Ctrl + L*
Blockquote	`> quote`	*Ctrl + Q*
H1	`# Heading`	*Ctrl + Alt + 1*
H2	`## Heading`	*Ctrl + Alt + 2*
H3	`### Heading`	*Ctrl + Alt + 3*
H4	`#### Heading`	*Ctrl + Alt + 4*
H5	`##### Heading`	*Ctrl + Alt + 5*

Result	Markdown	Shortcut
H6	`###### Heading`	*Ctrl + Alt + 6*
Select word		*Ctrl + Alt + W*
New paragraph		*Ctrl / Cmd + Enter*
Uppercase		*Ctrl + U*
Lowercase		*Ctrl + Shift + U*
Titlecase		*Ctrl + Alt + Shift + U*
Insert current date		*Ctrl + Shift + 1*

For further Markdown syntax reference:
Markdown Documentation

Index

Symbols

{{asset}} tag 77
{{author}} object
  properties 83
{{{body}}} tag 77
{{body_class}} tag 77
{{{body}}} tag 77
{{content}} tag 81, 105
{{date}} tag 80
{{!< default}} tag 79
{{#each}} helper 52
{{excerpt}} tag 81
{{#foreach posts}}...{{/foreach}} block
        helper tags 79
{{ghost_foot}} tag 78
{{ghost_head}} tag 77
{{pagination}} tag 81
{{post_class}} tag 80
{{{tags}}} tag 81
{{title}} tag 80
{{url}} tag 80

A

Amazon EC2
  Ghost, hosting on 25-27
author profile settings, Ghost 13, 14

B

basic code
  adding, to default.hbs file 75, 76
  adding, to index.hbs file 79
  adding, to page.hbs file 85
  adding, to post.hbs file 82
  adding, to tag.hbs file 84

blog, Ghost(Pro)
  general settings 11, 12
  settings, configuring 11
  user account, creating 9, 10
  user settings 12-14

C

CentOS, for VPS
  Ghost, configuring on 36
CentOS (VPS and local)
  Ghost, installing on 34-36
Command not found error 48
content blocks 113
content management
  about 14
  area 14, 15
  draft, saving 19
  existing posts, editing 17
  featured posts 17
  inline preview 18
  permalink, modifying 16
  post, converting to page 15, 16
  post editing area 18
  posts, creating 15
  posts, deleting 15
  post's permalink, modifying 22
  posts, publishing 20, 21
  posts, unpublishing 20, 21
  publishing date, modifying 16
  tags, adding 19
  title, setting 19
  word count display 20
CSS
  creating, via Stylus 54

current exclusions, Ghost
  comments 69
  menus 69
  sidebar widgets 69

D

default.hbs file
  {{{body}}} tag 77
  {{ghost_foot}} tag 78
  about 75, 76
  document <footer> section 78
  document <header> section 77, 78
  extra scripts 78
  wrapper code 77
default themes
  about 90
  blog cover image, using as
        site background 97-99
  single column 90-93
  twin column 94-96
design options, Ghost
  current exclusions 69
  primary theme design building blocks 67
  themeable areas 66
  tools 68
design tools
  @even 69
  @first 68
  {{#has}} helper 68
  @last 68
  @odd 69
  @rowEnd 69
  @rowStart 69
  columns 69
  Content blocks 68
  Featured post status 68
DigitalOcean
  about 26
  URL 26
double curly braces 51
draft
  saving 19

E

else helper 53
existing posts
  editing 17

F

foreach block helpers 52
forever list command 44
forever logs command 44
forever process manager
  about 43, 44
  URL 44
forever restartall command 44
forever stopall command 44

G

Ghost
  automated installation 7
  command-line interface 30
  configuring, on CentOS for VPS 36
  configuring, on OS X 37, 38
  configuring, on Ubuntu for VPS 34
  configuring, on Windows (local) 39, 40
  design options 66
  hosting 25
  hosting, on Amazon EC2 27
  hosting, on DigitalOcean 26
  inline HTML 24
  image, uploading 24
  installing, on CentOS (VPS and local) 34-36
  installing, on Mac OS X (local) 37
  installing, on Ubuntu (VPS and local) 32, 33
  installing, on Windows (local) 39
  manual installation 30
  Markdown syntax 131
  pricing chart, URL 9
  result 131
  shortcut keys 131
  SSH access 30, 31
  troubleshooting 47
  upgrading 46, 47
  URL 9, 46
  VPS operating system, identifying 31

Ghost(Pro)
  blog, creating 9
Ghost (VPS)
  custom domain, pointing at 41
Grunt
  installing 60

H

Handlebars
  logic-less templating 50
  URL 54
hosting solution, Ghost
  using 8, 9

I

icon fonts
  adding 116, 117
if helper 52
image fallbacks
  setting 117
import_stylus.styl file 88
index and tag archive
  excerpt 105
  featured posts 108, 109
  posts 105
  show post 105
  styles, applying to featured posts 109
  styles, applying to posts with
        certain tags 110-112
  zebra striping, adding 106-108
index.hbs file 79-81

J

JavaScript
  minifying 63

L

listen EADDRINUSE IN USE error 47
listen EADDRNOTAVAIL error 47
logic-less templating, Handlebars
  {{#each}} helper 52
  about 50
  comments 54
  double curly braces 51

else helper 53
foreach block helpers 52
if helper 52
paths 51
template tag parameters 54
triple curly braces 51
unless helper 53

M

Mac OS X (local)
  Ghost, installing on 37
  Ghost, configuring on 37, 38
Markdown
  about 22-24
  syntax 131
  URL 24
  using 23
meta content 77
meta folder 88
mixins 57, 58
multiple Ghost blogs
  hosting, on same VPS 42

N

Nginx 42

P

Package Control 59
package.json file 75
page.hbs file 85
post
  converting, to page 15, 16
  creating 15
  deleting 15
  publishing 20, 21
  techniques 115, 116
  unpublishing 20, 21
post.hbs file 82, 83
project compiler
  installing 61
project environment
  creating 60
  Grunt, installing 60
  JavaScript, minifying 63

Package Control 59
project compiler, installing 61
project folder, creating 61
project options, setting 62
setting up 58
Stylus, installing 59
Sublime Text 2 58
watch task, running 62
project folder
compiler 61
creating 61
js 61
stylus 61
project options
setting 62
Putty
URL 27, 30

Q

quick start theme quiz
about 69
default features 70
index and tag archive 70
post and page 71
post feature 72
tag archive 71
quick start theme quiz, choices
applying 90
default themes 90
index and tag archive 105
post and page 114
single column layout 100

S

Secure Shell (SSH) access 30
shortcut keys, Ghost 131
single column layout
full screen header 104
header height, automatic sizing 100, 101
header height, setting 102, 103
SSL
adding, for security 44, 45
styles
applying, to featured posts 109
applying, to posts with certain tags 110-112

styles folder
about 89
custom_classes.styl file 89
element_defaults.styl file 89
media_queries.styl file 89
Stylus
installing 59
mixins 57
syntax, using 56, 57
syntax, writing rules 57
variables, creating 55
Stylus files, working
about 88
import_stylus.styl file 88
meta folder 88
styles folder 89
vars_mixins_etc folder 89
Stylus syntax
using 56, 57
writing, rules 57
Sublime Text 2
about 58
URL 58

T

tag archives
about 114
styling 113
tag.hbs file 84
tags
adding 19
template tag parameters 54
test content
adding 85
theme
activating 85
themeable areas, Ghost blog
default 66
index 67
page 67
post 67
tag archive 67
theme shell
basic code, adding to template files 74
creating 72

CSS, running 74
folder structure 72, 73
JS compile, running 74
setup file 72, 73
title, post
setting 19
triple curly braces 51
troubleshooting
Command not found error 48
listen EADDRINUSE IN USE error 47
listen EADDRNOTAVAIL error 47
twin column design
media queries, adding 123-128
twin column visual styling 118-122

U

Ubuntu, for VPS
Ghost, configuring on 34
Ubuntu (VPS and local)
Ghost, installing on 32, 33
unique visual styling
adding 116
icon fonts, adding 116, 117
image fallbacks, setting 117
twin column visual styling 118
unless helper 53

V

vars_mixins_etc folder 89
Virtual Private Server (VPS)
about 26
configuration 41-46
operating system, identifying 31
Virtual Private Server (VPS), configuration
custom domain, pointing at Ghost (VPS) 41
forever process manager 43, 44
Ghost, running 43
Ghost, upgrading 46, 47
multiple Ghost blogs, hosting on
    same VPS 42
Nginx 42
SSL, adding for security 44, 45

W

watch task
running 62, 63
Windows (local)
Ghost, configuring on 39, 40
Ghost, installing on 39

Z

zebra striping
adding 106-108

Thank you for buying
Getting Started with Ghost

About Packt Publishing

Packt, pronounced 'packed', published its first book *"Mastering phpMyAdmin for Effective MySQL Management"* in April 2004 and subsequently continued to specialize in publishing highly focused books on specific technologies and solutions.

Our books and publications share the experiences of your fellow IT professionals in adapting and customizing today's systems, applications, and frameworks. Our solution based books give you the knowledge and power to customize the software and technologies you're using to get the job done. Packt books are more specific and less general than the IT books you have seen in the past. Our unique business model allows us to bring you more focused information, giving you more of what you need to know, and less of what you don't.

Packt is a modern, yet unique publishing company, which focuses on producing quality, cutting-edge books for communities of developers, administrators, and newbies alike. For more information, please visit our website: www.packtpub.com.

About Packt Open Source

In 2010, Packt launched two new brands, Packt Open Source and Packt Enterprise, in order to continue its focus on specialization. This book is part of the Packt Open Source brand, home to books published on software built around Open Source licenses, and offering information to anybody from advanced developers to budding web designers. The Open Source brand also runs Packt's Open Source Royalty Scheme, by which Packt gives a royalty to each Open Source project about whose software a book is sold.

Writing for Packt

We welcome all inquiries from people who are interested in authoring. Book proposals should be sent to author@packtpub.com. If your book idea is still at an early stage and you would like to discuss it first before writing a formal book proposal, contact us; one of our commissioning editors will get in touch with you.

We're not just looking for published authors; if you have strong technical skills but no writing experience, our experienced editors can help you develop a writing career, or simply get some additional reward for your expertise.

Getting Started with SOQL

ISBN: 978-1-78328-735-2   Paperback: 130 pages

Revolutionize the use of simple query strings to make them more efficient using SOQL

1. Write optimized SOQL statements.

2. Discover the standards to follow while writing SOQL statements.

3. Learn how to write SOQL statements without hitting the limits set by Salesforce.com.

Magento Responsive Theme Design

ISBN: 978-1-78398-036-9   Paperback: 110 pages

Leverage the power of Magento to successfully develop and deploy a responsive Magento theme

1. Build a mobile-, tablet-, and desktop-friendly e-commerce site.

2. Refine your Magento store's product and category pages for mobile.

3. Easy-to-follow, step-by-step guide on how to get up and running with Magento.

Please check **www.PacktPub.com** for information on our titles

WordPress Web Application Development

ISBN: 978-1-78328-075-9   Paperback: 376 pages

Develop powerful web applications quickly using cutting-edge WordPress web development techniques

1. Develop powerful web applications rapidly with WordPress.

2. Practical scenario-based approach with ready-to-test source code.

3. Learn how to plan complex web applications from scratch.

Instant Brainshark

ISBN: 978-1-78355-926-8   Paperback: 52 pages

Convert your boring, outdated slideshows into engaging and powerful audio presentations using Brainshark

1. Learn something new in an Instant! A short, fast, focused guide delivering immediate results.

2. Master the basics of Brainshark to get started immediately.

3. Learn how to share your Brainshark presentation on over 100 social media websites.

4. Written in an easy-to-read style which allows anybody to become productive quickly.

Please check **www.PacktPub.com** for information on our titles